PROUST AND VENICE

J. Ruskin, *St Mark's, Venice,* Brantwood.

PROUST AND VENICE

Peter Collier

66, 694

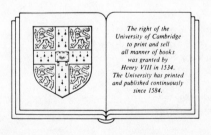

The right of the
University of Cambridge
to print and sell
all manner of books
was granted by
Henry VIII in 1534.
The University has printed
and published continuously
since 1584.

CAMBRIDGE UNIVERSITY PRESS

Cambridge
New York   Port Chester
Melbourne   Sydney

Published by the Press Syndicate of the University of Cambridge
The Pitt Building, Trumpington Street, Cambridge CB2 IRP
40 West 20th Street, New York, NY 10011, USA
10 Stamford Road, Oakleigh, Melbourne 3166, Australia

Originally published in Italian (translated by Daniela Fink) as *Mosaici Proustiani*

by Società Editrice Il Mulino 1986
and © Società Editrice Il Mulino 1986

This edition first published in English by Cambridge University Press 1989 as
Proust and Venice

English translation © Cambridge University Press 1989

Printed in Great Britain at The Bath Press, Avon

British Library cataloguing in publication data

Collier, Peter, *1942–*
Proust and Venice.
1. Fiction in French. Proust, Marcel, 1871–1922. – Critical Studies
I. Title   II. Mosaici Proustiani. *English*
843′.912

Library of Congress cataloguing in publication data
Collier, Peter.
Proust and Venice / Peter Collier.
     p.   cm.
Bibliography.
Includes index.
ISBN 0 521 36206 7
1. Proust, Marcel, 1871–1922 – Knowledge – Italy – Venice.
2. Proust, Marcel, 1871–1922 – Knowledge – Art.
3. Venice (Italy) in literature.
4. Art in literature.   5. Art – Italy – Venice.
I. Title.
PQ2631.R63Z545984   1989
843′.912 – dc20   89–31451   CIP

ISBN 0 521 36206 7

Contents

Illustrations

Acknowledgements

I am grateful to the following for permission to reproduce illus-
trations: The Brantwood Trust, Coniston (frontispiece), L'Accademia, Venice (1, 2, 5, 7, 8, 9, 10), Musei Civici di Padova (3), Museo
Fortuny, Venice (4, 11, 12), Mauritshuis, The Hague (13), Scuola
Dalmata dei SS. Giorgio e Trifone (14); to Osvaldo Böhm for his
photography (1, 2, 5, 7, 8, 9, 10, 14); and to The British Academy
and Cambridge University for research grants. I also wish to thank
most warmly all those colleagues who offered advice at various stages
of my research and writing, including Malcolm Bowie, Patrick
Boyde, Alison Finch, Daniela Fink, Carola Hicks, Vivien Law, Tony
Tanner, Jeremy Whiteley. Finally, this book could never have been
written without the unstinting generosity, support and affection of
Giulio Lucchetta and Paola Masat. I dedicate it to them, with these
words by Proust: 'Tout comme l'avenir, ce n'est pas tout à la fois,
mais grain par grain qu'on goûte le passé.'

Abbreviations

Page references in the text observe the following conventions. For *A la recherche du temps perdu* reference is made to the Kilmartin translation (K, followed by volume and page numbers), and the Pléiade edition of the French text P, followed by volume and page numbers). I have referred to the 1954 edition rather than to the new edition in process of publication, because the 1954 edition will be more readily available in libraries for some time to come, and because Kilmartin's translation uses the 1954 text). In referring to *Contre Sainte-Beuve*, I distinguish between the editions by B de Fallois (*CSB* F) and the Pléiade edition (*CSB* P), with the appropriate translation from *On Reading Ruskin* (*ORR*) or *By Way of Sainte-Beuve* (*BWSB*), where available (different selections of texts appear in the various editions). Any translations not otherwise attributed are my own. On one or two rare occasions I have slightly amended the excellent Kilmartin translation where a point in my commentary required it. I have referred to Proust's original volumes with their French titles (e.g., *A l'ombre des jeunes filles en fleurs*), rather than use the versions consecrated by Scott Montcrieff (e.g., *Within a Budding Grove*).

Introduction

> Les beaux livres sont écrits dans une sorte de langue
> étrangère. Sous chaque mot chacun de nous met son sens
> ou du moins son image qui est souvent un contre-sens.
>
> Marcel Proust

A la recherche du temps perdu is the record of a long voyage of discovery, a journey towards the reconstitution of the fragmented self,
the key to whose wholeness is revealed when in the last volume,
Le temps retrouvé, the hero Marcel stumbles on a paving stone one
morning in Paris, and this sensory experience brings back the forgotten experience of walking on the uneven flagstones of the Baptistery
of St Mark's Basilica in Venice. From this moment, Marcel's shattered self is reconstituted like a mosaic. In fact he had long fantasised
a journey to Venice as the ultimate cultural experience, but, like
other dream figures – the novelist Bergotte, the painter Elstir, the
aristocratic Guermantes family, girls like Gilberte and then Albertine
– Venice was a source of disappointment as much as of experience
when it was finally attained, in *La Fugitive*.

As Proust's hero Marcel searches for a meaning to the world and
to himself, he follows a circular Odyssey, from his childish literary
dreams in the village of Combray, to the final adult fictionalisation
of his childhood visions, in the novel which the mature Marcel
decides to write at the end of *A la recherche du temps perdu*. During
this adventure, there is a constant process of projection and displacement of potentially enlightening structures. Society, love, literature
and even the city of Venice are invested with emotional and heuristic
value, only to be drained of their plenitude, to be rejected as hollow,
meaningless experience or unassimilable, grotesque motifs.

Ultimately, it is a cluster of works located in or inspired by Venice

I

(dresses, paintings, frescoes, buildings, mosaics) which provides the key to the subjective structure of reality and meaning. In our journey through the text we meet a series of epiphanies and motifs which radiate structural significance. A Giotto fresco, a Carpaccio painting, a Fortuny dress, a mosaic or a flagstone, are no longer symbolic in the allegorical way of nineteenth-century French symbolism. They are motifs whose internal and contextual structuring implies similar structuring in the growing narratorial and textual consciousness enveloping them.

Proust, like Freud, used the image of archeology to express the conflictual, spatial layering of time in the mind, and in Proust, as in Freud's *Interpretation of Dreams*, there are spatial condensations, and displacements of images and sensations, interferences between different levels of time and consciousness. But Proust's text provides both the narrative of the dream and its recall, both its original scenario and its secondary revision: everything that the dreamer's devious mind secretes is ingested by the text into one of its growing crystalline structures. Proust's text is thus one of those privileged literary spaces which provide the reader with a complex labyrinth of imaginative experience and also the thread of consciousness with which to explore it. The text is at once the record of a long, opaque, imaginative adventure, and the reorganised, reinterpreted life structured by the theory of consciousness and aesthetics which is discovered in that search.

One of Proust's most typical structures, in this circular exploration by the mind of its own imagery, which in its turn reflects the outside world, is the *mise en abyme*, a representation in miniature of an image or a form embedded within the framework of a similar, but larger structure. My book explores the ways in which Proust's text focuses on Venice and Venetian art, or their Ruskinian reflections, in order to create its vital circular model of consciousness which mediates feeling through memory and recreates it in art. I shall now resume the stages of my own Venetian research.

Proust himself travelled little, although he did visit the cathedrals and churches of Normandy, inspired by Ruskin's *Bible of Amiens* and *Sesame and Lilies*, which he translated. But his interest in John Ruskin and Emile Mâle, whose studies of the survival of medieval motif through the medium of art may have helped Proust evolve his theory of involuntary memory, also led him to make a cultural pilgrimage to the Venice celebrated by Ruskin (although Proust did not do this until after Ruskin's death in 1900). Ruskin had criticised art which preferred aesthetic beauty to religious morality or truth. Proust, whose *Recherche* proposes a system in which art becomes a transcendental value, argues, in the prefaces to his Ruskin translations, that Ruskin himself tends to prefer artistic erudition to artistic sincerity. Such excessive erudition, which Proust calls idolatry, borrowing the very term which Ruskin used differently, is a constant feature of *A la recherche du temps perdu*. In the first volume, *Du côté de chez Swann*, the amateur art-historian Charles Swann acts as mentor and alter ego of the young hero Marcel, just as Ruskin's writings had for Proust. Yet Swann, despite his artistic pretensions, fails to create or even fully interpret art. Vermeer's, Botticelli's and Giotto's paintings, and the music of Proust's imaginary musician, Vinteuil, obsess him, but insight into their form and their spiritual and emotional power finally eludes him. He falls victim to a search for wit and erudition in their own right, scoring social successes with his comments on Giotto, finding erotic excitement by relating his mistress Odette to a figure painted by Botticelli, but failing to plumb the meaning of the original works. Marcel, too, seeks authority in the opinions of a critic, Swann, a novelist, Bergotte, or a fictitious painter, Elstir in *A l'ombre des jeunes filles en fleurs*, as well as in their artistry. Venice is the epitome of his search, as it seems to contain the ultimate in painting, sculpture and architecture.

For the adolescent Marcel, in *Du côté de chez Swann*, Venice is initially a fantasised topos of cultural and sexual fulfilment. Swann gives him reproductions of Giotto's figures of the *Vices and Virtues* from the Cappella degli Scrovegni (Proust having annexed Giotto and Padua to the Venetian tourist circuit). But Marcel becomes so excited at the idea of being taken to Venice, that he makes himself too ill to go. Later, as a young man living with his mistress, Albertine, his cultural urge to attain Venice increases; *La prisonnière* shows him thinking of the Titians he could see there, but his liaison with Albertine and his desire for Venice are mutually incompatible: he dare not leave her to possible infidelity in Paris, nor dare he take her with him to intrude upon the erotic opportunities of the exotic city of Venice. He tries to compromise by creating a conflation of erotic and cultural Venetian imagery, draping Albertine in gowns bought from the Venetian designer Fortuny: which render her sexually attractive but simultaneously evoke the imagery of Carpaccio's paintings. Then her death renders the whole erotic and cultural Venetian complex as it were taboo – until, in *La fugitive*, Marcel's mother, excluded previously by the illicit affair, fulfils her maternal desire by taking her son to the forbidden city. On Marcel's arrival, Venice creates its own works of art from its canals, gondolas and palaces, as well as opening up its museums, and yet he can also indulge in the pursuit of local girls. This desire at first revives a nostalgic feeling for Albertine, but the images of his desire are later liberated from the image of Albertine, when she is finally released from the prison of Marcel's memory (figured as the *piombi* and *pozzi* of Venice), by linguistic and visual accidents, including the eagle of St John, associated with Albertine because of the eagle motif on the rings which she had been given by another admirer. The hero finally works on Ruskin and art in the presence of his mother in the Baptistery of St Mark's, in a scene of great import, since the return of this scene via involuntary memory, in *Le temps retrouvé*, triggered when Marcel trips over a paving stone in Paris, will provide him with the revelation of the meaning of his life and the means of its salvation through art. Venice, after being a chimerical erotic and cultural ideal in *Du côté de chez Swann* and *La prisonnière*, becomes in *La fugitive* a latent figure of Marcel's memory and creativity.

Much of Proust's writing treats reality as if it were a text, knowledge a textual critique, and art a series of intertextual structures. In *A l'ombre des jeunes filles en fleurs*, Albertine and her band of girlfriends on holiday at the seaside are described in terms of Bellini angels, using terminology derived from Ruskin. In *Le côté de Guermantes*, amid Marcel's long excursion into the Parisian upper classes, we see Swann reduced to purveying idolatrous iconography, when a vast photograph of a Venetian coin, acquired in order to flatter the aristocratic Guermantes family's genealogical vanity, represents a grotesque and empty inflation of the postcard reproductions of Giotto which he had previously offered the young Marcel. A quotation from Vergil, originally borrowed by Ruskin and now adapted by Swann, shows Swann's surreptitious contempt for the Guermantes and his acknowledgement of approaching death. Later, in *La fugitive*, the shift in gender of a quotation from Racine's *Phèdre* will suggest Marcel's jealousy and Albertine's bisexuality. These quotations are incorporated into the fabric of Proust's text, I argue, just as Ruskin says mosaics are incrusted into Venetian buildings, so that they become part of its significant structure.

Proust develops other passages from Ruskin's work on Venice, some of which he ironically renders deliberately more romantic than the original, and he develops odd insights of Ruskin, such as the discovery in *Du côté de chez Swann* that a Turneresque lagoon lies embedded in a Titian townscape of Venice, confirming Marcel's grandmother's view of the many-layered nature of art, and preparing us for the resurrection through art of the narrator's experience. In *La fugitive*, Ruskin's depictions of blue shadows in terms of water, and of yellow stone as petrified sunlight, are modulated by Proust; the fields of Combray are rewritten in the marine terms of Venice, and the church of Combray (already seen as a boat in *Du côté de chez Swann*) becomes the great marine vessel of St Mark's. In *Le temps retrouvé* Proust's pastiche of the Goncourt Journal, relating the use of a Sansovino well as an ashtray, is perhaps inspired by Ruskin's criticism of the industrialisation of Venice, with its desecration of Venetian art. In *A l'ombre des jeunes filles en fleurs*, the pretentious Bloch mocks Venetian tourism – but his comments are taken from Ruskin's own reaction to the vulgarisation of *The Stones of Venice*. In all of these examples, Ruskin's original text is lovingly recomposed, reformulated and transformed in the Proustian mosaic.

As Marcel's grandmother prefers landscapes made artistic by preservation in a painting embedded in its turn by an engraving, so Proust in *Du côté de chez Swann* uses Gentile Bellini's painting of the mosaic arch of St Mark's which figures in miniature the whole surrounding basilica. Proust explores its infinite regression, showing that it is through *mise en abîme* that art is preserved, embedded in layers of representation just as experience is embedded in memory. Artistic form is often used to envelop experience in *A la recherche du temps perdu.* In *La prisonnière* Proust uses comparisons between Mantegna and Bellini, between different musical instruments, and between music and painting, in order to compare two different works by his imaginery composer, Vinteuil, and their psychological effects on the listener. In *A l'ombre des jeunes filles en fleurs*, a departure by train is compared to a Mantegna crucifixion, to Dante's *Inferno* or to an Impressionist painting, projecting emotion as something both aesthetic and metaphysical, parallel with artistic experience.

Artistic models of feeling and knowledge are developed self-consciously by Proust's characters. Marcel proves to be more sophisticated than Swann in exploiting Giotto's image of Charity in *Du côté de chez Swann*, and develops his own interpretation of Giotto's Envy in *Le côté de Guermantes*, as a figure of divided or circular consciousness – the consciousness of the dreamer or the artist himself. The topos of Venice is explored as a model of consciousness containing the unknown: Venetian motifs of glass and water present the structure of consciousness reflecting its own unconscious depth. In *La fugitive* painting is also used as a model of *mise en abîme*: Marcel observing girls at windows in Venice appears framed by their vision, as Venice is contained within a painting by Carpaccio; in *Du côté de chez Swann*, Swann was similarly engulfed by the structure of the Vinteuil melody he was listening to, as the observer of a de Hooch painting is overrun by its reechoing framing devices. Again Marcel creates a more sophisticated aesthetic structure to express emotional experience than Swann: glassblowing and mosaic are used as *mises en abîme* of the very text of *La fugitive*, which is being created by the narrator. In *La fugitive* Marcel also sees himself as a new Scheherezade from the *Arabian Nights* – evoked by the Oriental associations of Venice – reflecting the way his self is caught up in and structured by his own narrative at the same time as it creates that narrative.

But the most complex cultural model of the *mise en abîme* is created by Proust in Fortuny's dresses, first evoked by the painter Elstir in *A l'ombre des jeunes filles en fleurs*, with their deliberate reference to an Oriental and cultural as well as an erotic Venice. In *La prisonnière* Marcel dresses Albertine in gowns which recall Venetian buildings, Italian libraries and Arabic script. Proust multiplies references to the phoenix, a motif on the dresses, linking it with the thematics of resurrection, no doubt inspired by the presence in Venetian architecture of a similar motif, that of the peacock. Proust appears to have invented his own Fortuny dresses with phoenix or peacock motifs, and evokes disturbing movements of the birds on the folds of the dresses in order to suggest a link between sexuality and death. The way in which an artistic motif can resurrect experience is further shown when a Combray church which was like a peacock's tail in *Du côté de chez Swann*, and the peacock-tail ocean of Balbec, described in *A l'ombre des jeunes filles en fleurs*, are revived in the context of Marcel's recall of Venice in *Le temps retrouvé*, inspired by the sight of a stiffly displayed table-napkin. Moreover, the self-reflexive mirroring of the artist through such motifs is figured in the enigmatic twin eagles on one of Albertine's rings, whose equivocal image echoes the puzzled face of Marcel, who hopes by scrutinising that image to decode the identity of the amorous donor of the ring, and the nature of Albertine's unorthodox infidelity, confirmed posthumously in *La fugitive*. In *La fugitive*, too, an eagle motif is found at S. Giorgio degli Schiavoni, beside paintings by Carpaccio, and it is in connection with such paintings and motifs seen in Venice, that Albertine appears to be raised from the dead. But Marcel cannot entirely retrieve and master her lost image from his past because he cannot at this stage revive and recreate his own past. Proust's whole text suggests that the bodily has to be transcended, has to be translated into form, in order that the spiritual be reborn. The intertwined birds everywhere present in St Mark's Basilica reveal the same message of desire transcended and resurrection prefigured.

But above all Proust uses Carpaccio's painting as a model of his own text. In *La prisonnière* he analyses the *mise en abîme* of Carpaccio's *Incontro die fidanzati*, from the *Sant' Orsola* cycle. The constitutive differences of sea and land are transgressed, as they were in Elstir's paintings in *A l'ombre des jeunes filles en fleurs*, in order, according to Elstir himself, to found a theory of metaphor. The structures of Carpaccio's castles, galleons and bridges re-echo each other, as the self-reflexive dreamer in the *Sogno di S. Orsola* and the scribe in the *Congedo degli ambasciatori inglesi* echo the self-productive structuring of the painter, or writer. Similarly, in *Le côté de Guermantes*, the duc de Guermantes' past is embedded in his discourse in a way which reminds the narrator of Carpaccio's mutually embedded narratives. The structure of memory, through intricate cross-referencing of motifs and themes, functions like a work of art. In *La prisonnière* Marcel notes, in connection with the Fortuny phenomenon, how Christ's resurrection is resurrected in its turn through the imagery of the mosaics of St Mark's – their iconography and legends. The bird imagery of the church also revives for the narrator the stained-glass windows of the church in Combray, as that of the dresses resurrects the Venetian imagery of Carpaccio's painting, like a reliquary preserving a precious material, which in its turn preserved a precious relic. Fortuny revives in his dresses the visions of Carpaccio, after Carpaccio had preserved artistic motifs in his paintings as if in a reliquary. The dress revives a painting which preserved the dress of its times, and the painting evoked by the dress thus evokes images of Venetian painting in general: the dresses are an image of an image, a metaphor of a metaphor. The accidental transmission of art through non-artistic – in this case religious – practice is suggested by Proust. In Christian reliquaries, in Carpaccio's paintings and in Fortuny's dresses, the container of the relic becomes the contained, becomes in fact the artistic relic. The text creating Combray in *Du côté de chez Swann* embeds the local church of St Hilaire, then the text itself becomes a cathedral, the book having evolved from within this architectural structure. In *Le temps retrouvé* Marcel compares his writing not only to such a cathedral, but also to dressmaking, involving patchwork, expansion and reinforcing through cross-reference and motif.

According to Emile Mâle, an art-historian with whom Proust corresponded, medieval French religious sculpture copied grotesque motifs from Islamic or Byzantine cloth, including the double-headed eagle and the intertwined peacocks. A captured military flag, for instance, was mistakenly preserved in a church as a religious relic, and functioned unwittingly as the reliquary of an artistic motif. Oriental cloths hung in churches had their motifs transposed into the more permanent fabric of mosaic floors, or stained-glass windows. I argue that Proust appears to have appropriated this model. According to his own text, the death of the substance of the original experience is required, so that its aesthetic structure will survive in more enduring form. Thus the contingent sensory experience and mnemonic patterns of *A la recherche du temps perdu* become both the content and the form of the finished work.

Proust exploits all the historical, religious and artistic overtones of St Mark's Basilica in Venice to structure his model of art and memory preserving experience. When Marcel arrives in Venice, in *La fugitive*, the whole of Combray is regenerated in Proust's description of Venice, as the primitive St Theodore is regenerated in the more modern patron Saint of Venice, St Mark, and the church becomes a gospel, prefiguring Marcel's own book, as the pure golden angel of the Campanile welcomes Marcel after the disappearance of the more fleshly embracings of Albertine, in *La prisonnière*. But Albertine too had had her spiritual and artistic dimension even in her erotic beauty, with her resemblance to a carved wooden angel. Marcel's erotic knowledge of her in *La prisonnière* prepared in him her spiritual transformation through memory in *La fugitive*, where she takes on a role purified and sanctified by implicit comparison to Mary Magdalene in allusions to Carpaccio's paintings. The mother figure in the *Martirio e funerali di S. Orsola* appears to echo the posture of the Virgin Mary in the Baptistery mosaics, and Marcel's own mother in the Baptistery appears to pray for her son, as if she were presiding over his redemption as a man and his rebirth as an artist. The Baptistery mosaics of rebirth, and the statue of John the Baptist on the font, appear to promise revival, even as the figure of the latter appears to repress the memory of Albertine. The mother-figure is consecrated as a medium of artistic experience, becoming part of the mosaic of memory, watching over Marcel like Mary over Christ, as Marcel in the very Baptistery commits himself to the act of writing. The artistry of memory is seen as a mosaic which will also preserve the figure of the mother.

Although the configuration of the mosaic as *mise en abîme* of art and experience seems now to assume its full significance, Marcel's quest is still incomplete at this point in *La fugitive*, because of his idolatrous over-dependence on Ruskin, whom he studies in the heart of the Baptistery. Yet it is the Baptistery topos which will eventually be resurrected in *Le temps retrouvé* (it is the Baptistery floor which will be reactivated by Marcel stumbling over a paving stone outside the Guermantes' residence in Paris), because it is the moment of the narrator's rebirth of creativity through writing, and its linkage with memory structures a revision of personal experience.

Resurrection through writing and its accidental retexturing of private experience had already been signalled in *La prisonnière*, where the dying novelist Bergotte envied the genius of Vermeer, who captured the texture of lived experience in his *View of Delft*, irrespective of his conscious plan to paint a realistic landscape. Bergotte does not realise that he too has transposed experience into texture, independently of the planned subject of his novels, although the young Marcel who read his works in *Du côté de chez Swann* spontaneously read them for their evocative style rather than their overt message. Marcel's own art will be a retranslation of the lived experience of Venice, among other places and events. Marcel, as Ruskin says of Dandolo in his Baptistery tomb, is a sleeper at the heart of his petrified creation, the dreamer Marcel being overlooked by Ruskin as John the Baptist overlooks the apparently sleeping Dandolo. Proust's dreamer at the heart of his *Recherche*, exploring his own circular consciousness, is also like Dante at the heart of his *Commedia*, whose fantastic visions both inform and are created by him. If my quest for Proust's *Recherche* focuses finally on a Florentine, transported like Giotto by Proust to the heart of a Venetian experience, it is no doubt that my Italy, like Proust's, is less a place than a *cosa mentale*. But it also shows the ambition of Proust to relate his personal insights to the greatest literature of all time, as it is my ambition to show that Proust's exploration of Venice and Venetian artefacts opens out into a universally valid aesthetic, regenerating all our experience through the structures of memory, perception and art. My conclusion shows how that structure is generated and performed at the very heart of the Proustian sentence.

I
Proust's travels; 'Impossible venir, mensonge suit'

> La présence, en écartant de nous la seule réalité, celle qu'on pense, adoucit les souffrances, et l'absence les ranime.
> Marcel Proust

On 14 July 1902 the Campanile in Saint Mark's square, Venice, collapsed, after being for centuries one of the most famous landmarks in Europe. The municipal council decreed that it should be reconstructed, stone by stone, 'com' era, dov' era' – as it was, where it was.[1]

The pulverisation of a structure, followed by a reconstruction meticulous enough to count as a resurrection, is also an image of Proust's *A la Recherche du temps perdu*. Enormous mental and social constructions – love, art, history, society – are elaborated in the course of the *Recherche*, only to crumble to dust. Meanwhile, the novel keeps hinting at some miraculous resuscitation of the lost experience. But Proust's transcendental recuperation of his experience at the end of *Le Temps retrouvé*, like the kaleidoscope or the mosaic, is both a total rearrangement of the fragments of that experience, and an artistic preservation of their fragmentary integrity. Proust's reconstruction is both creation and salvation through the medium of an aesthetic reworking of superficially non-aesthetic experience. Hence the particular importance of references to works of art throughout the *Recherche*, and the significance of Venice – the artistic Mecca for Proust as for so many art-lovers – as the substance of Marcel's final revelation, as well as one of the main artistic motifs binding together various aesthetic intuitions of Marcel throughout the novel.

Venice, for the real Marcel Proust, was at once a most desired and yet an almost forbidden city. Strangely, he made no attempt to visit it during his first year's work translating Ruskin, but he did compensate by making a short trip with his mother in May 1900, after a brief flurry of hagiographic correspondence with Marie Nordlinger (a young English sculptor, related to Proust's friend Reynaldo Hahn) about Ruskin, after his death in January 1900.[2] It is as if the living presence of Ruskin prevented Proust from visiting the city which he imagined so powerfully from Ruskin's writings.

Proust's withdrawal from travel is splendidly comic. He forbids himself Florence for fear of provoking his asthma, yet Florence in winter would probably have been no more pollenated than Venice in May.[3] He was actually quite ill in Venice, so it appears.[4] As for other destinations, a hilarious ballet of telegrams misconstrued or mistransmitted is organised by Proust, so that his protestations of willingness to meet Antoine Bibesco in Munich or in Constantinople are always perfectly unsynchronised with their interlocutor's messages of courteous belief in the imminent arrival of Proust.[5] That Proust himself only half-believed in his own good faith in the matter is suggested by the typical apologetic telegram as propounded by the duc de Guermantes: 'Cannot come, lie follows' (K III 721, P III 703).

When he did visit Venice with his mother in May 1900 and met Marie Nordlinger and Reynaldo Hahn there, and when he went again in October 1900,[6] there is a sudden silence in his correspondance, as there was when he went to Holland in 1902. No card or letter seems to have been received by anyone from Venice, and only the odd postcard from Holland attests his disappointment with secular Flemish art after his indoctrination in Ruskinian religious art.[7] The main reason for the silence seems to be that he was occupied in intense activity, walking systematically around the monuments and museums, pausing only to read with Marie Nordlinger appropriate passages from Ruskin while stationed inside Saint Mark's Baptistery.[8]

For Proust himself at this stage, although he knew Ruskin's work on Italy well, the main relevance of Ruskin was as an interpreter of French Gothic, and his work on *La Bible d'Amiens* caused him to seek out anything by Ruskin on French cathedrals to the exclusion

of nearly all interest in Italy. As he approaches the end of his translation, he makes the tendentious comment that this work is finished.[9]
This double death, of the critic Ruskin and of his commentator
and translator Proust, accords with an impression that Venice was
not at this stage an overt force in Proust's life.

And two years later a significant moment occurs when he feels
that the labour of translation and commentary has been sterile: at
the moment of its completion he dismisses it as documentation rather
than creation. This very judgement however shows that with the
death of Ruskin and then of Proust's passion for working on Ruskin
comes the birth of a fragile urge to establish his own creative
originality.[10] When, in the course of the year 1900, he twice
accomplished the Ruskinian pilgrimage to Venice, he never quite
succumbed fully to Ruskin's idolatrous vision of this holy city of
art. In Swann's obsessive but incomplete study of Vermeer, and
in Bloch's attack on Ruskinian tours of 'Venice', we see echoes of
Proust's process of distancing himself from Ruskinian 'idolatry'.[11]
Nonetheless, after the publication of *La Bible d'Amiens* in 1904,
Proust went on to translate *Sesame and Lilies*, which he thought
an inferior work, and was not finally free of Ruskin until its publication in 1906.

Proust saw Ruskin as the indispensable guide to Venice, and, in
a rather extravagant conceit, went so far as to say that Ruskin had
changed its stones into bread, and this bread into roses.[12] Strangely,
however, considering the years Proust spent translating *The Bible
of Amiens* and *Sesame and Lilies*, and the proliferation of references
to Venice in *La Recherche*, there are very few overt references to
Ruskin in Proust's novel. Jupien refers to Marcel's translation of
Sesame and Lilies in *Le Temps retrouvé* (K III 862, P III 833); Marcel's
mother refers to Ruskin's 'voyageur ravi' in *A l'Ombre des jeunes
filles en fleurs* when Marcel is reluctant to leave her to go to Balbec;
Bloch mocks Marcel's desire to see Venice and sees it as a naive
Ruskinian romanticism (K I 794–5, P I 739); and one moment
of Marcel's search hints at a less ironic relationship, when Marcel
in *La Fugitive* enters St Mark's Baptistery to work on Ruskin (K
III 660, P III 645). And yet, as Elizabeth Jackson has shown, Proust's
theory of involuntary memory was largely evolved while and
through working on Ruskin.[13]

Proust's ambivalence towards Ruskin understandably runs deep throughout this time. Despite the fulsome rhetoric of his consolation of Antoine Bibesco for his mother's death in 1902, Proust seems sincere in quoting Ruskin as the only adequate expression of grief.[14] A little later, in 1903, Proust appears to pick up and complete the work on Ruskin, so often allegedly near completion but perpetually delayed, in a last effort of the will paying homage to his recently dead father, since his mother says he would have wanted Proust to finish it. Here the implication is that Proust can only consummate the work when the tutelary but intimidating figure of his father, who must have wanted his son's artistic activities to be given respectability through publication, was safely removed.[15]

An amusing echo of this complex relationship with his father may possibly be found in the *Recherche*, when Marcel learns from Mme de Villeparisis that his father (who has announced that he and Norpois have lost their luggage during an official trip to Spain, and will be delayed) has used this excuse in order to have an extra day's stay in Toledo to see El Greco's paintings: 'But he's anxious to spend a day longer in Toledo, since he's an admirer of a pupil of Titian – I forget the name – whose work can only be seen properly there.' (K 1 753, P 1 701). In *Combray* the father was the lawgiver and sacrificer, characterised at one moment as the figure of Abraham sacrificing his son Isaac in a painting by Bennozzo Gozzoli (K 1 39, P 1 36–7). Now in *A l'Ombre des jeunes filles en fleurs*, he is revealed to be evading the path of righteousness, deceiving his family and country in the pursuit of art, dallying with Titian's pupil in the same way that the son himself dreams of Titian and an artistic vocation and fails to renounce his mother's bedtime kiss with the stoicism demanded by his father. The father suddenly becomes human, artistic, morally fallible, but he is simultaneously viewed as more than human, as magnified by Mme de Villeparisis's interest, so that he is likened by Marcel to the figure of Jupiter in a painting by Gustave Moreau (K 1 754, P 1 701). We would now expect him to be more sympathetic to Marcel's artistic vocation, but, by the same token, we would expect Marcel's internalised image of his father's expectations to become all the more influential. Proust does not develop this insight – it remains an isolated flash of coincidence between the young artist and the overpowering father-figure, who are generally shown failing to communicate. Perhaps something of Proust's need to gain his father's posthumous respect, and to struggle free of the father-figure Ruskin, are reflected in this amusing episode. Perhaps this episode is also significant in showing the power of art to create sympathy even between those morally separated. At all events, Ruskin and Proust both treat art so reverently in their works that it tends to take on the role of an ethic or even a religion. Ruskin and Proust realise, however, how tendentious this is. Ruskin's own view of aesthetics was that beauty arose from sincere and good feelings: for him, 'idolatry' occurs when we idolise an artistic object independently of its spiritual import. He is very close to the traditional Biblical attack on 'graven images' (although he did prefer what he saw as a sincere, if misguided Catholic dependency on mediatory imagery to extremes of unemotional and theoretical belief in Protestant iconoclasm).

But in his preface to *La Bible d'Amiens* Proust moves away from Ruskin's critique of those who idolise art at the expense of a religious truth to which it should be subservient. Proust sees the clash latent within every artist, but he sees the terms of the conflict less as religious truth versus artistic beauty, than as the artist's own moral sincerity and internal truth versus his aesthetic form, which tends to become a superior reality:

We shall see that though the beauty in it is *in theory* (that is to say, in appearance, the basis of the writer's thought having always been appearance, and the form, reality) subordinated to moral feeling and truth, in reality truth and moral feeling are there subordinated to aesthetic feelings.

(*ORR* 51, *CSB* P 131).

Proust sees Ruskin himself as racked by the tension between his desires for beauty and for sincerity, 'humiliating beauty before duty, even if it were unaesthetic' (*ORR* 50, *CSB* P 130).

Proust admits the piety of Ruskin's overt argument, but discovers idolatry in the artistry of his arguments and his prose style:

At the very moment he was preaching sincerity, he was himself lacking in it, not by what he said, but by the way in which he said it. The doctrines he professed were moral doctrines and not aesthetic doctrines, and yet he chose them for their beauty. And since he did not wish to present them as beautiful but as true, he was forced to deceive himself about the nature of the reasons that made him adopt them.   (*ORR* 50–1, *CSB* P 130).

And very soon Proust has perversely relocated Ruskin's debate within an entirely aesthetic field, contrasting an *aesthetic* sincerity with the second-degree, self-conscious pleasure of *aesthetic* erudition:

In the same manner as the joy of seeing the beautiful, mysterious figures increased, but was altered in some way by the pleasure of erudition that I experienced upon understanding the text that had appeared in Byzantine letters around their haloed brows, so in the same way the beauty of Ruskin's images was intensified and corrupted by the pride of referring to the sacred text. A sort of egotistical self-evaluation is unavoidable in those joys in which erudition and art mingle and in which aesthetic pleasure may become more acute, but not remain as pure.   (*ORR* 53, *CSB* P 133).

This is almost a total reversal of Ruskin's basic proposition (based on the tension between spiritual truth and artistic beauty) – Proust redefines sincerity as *artistic* sincerity and sees aesthetic knowledge itself as a threat to pure, formal beauty. In so doing he admits that he is himself struggling with 'my most cherished aesthetic impressions' rather than 'wanting to denounce a personal fault' (*ORR* 54, *CSB* P 134).

His theory, as well as being personal and aesthetic, rather than Ruskinian and religious, is now more applicable to the art critic than to the artist or the general public, since excessive erudition has become the main component of idolatry. And indeed, in the same article on 'John Ruskin', Proust chooses his friend comte Robert de Montesquiou as the exemplary idolater (although he does not in this article mention him by name):

he recognizes admirably in the material with which a tragic actress drapes herself, the very fabric seen on *la Mort* in *Le Jeune Homme et la Mort*, by Gustave Moreau, or in the garb of one of his lady friends, "the very dress and coiffure worn by the princess de Cadignan the day she saw d'Arthez for the first time." And looking at the actress's draped costume or at the society lady's dress, touched by the nobility of his recollection he exclaims: "It is truly beautiful!" not because the fabric is beautiful, but because it is the fabric painted by Moreau or described by Balzac and is thus forever sacred ... to the idolaters.   (*ORR* 55–6, *CSB* P 135).

Proust rather rashly dissociates himself from this hagiographic approach to art, claiming that he will not allow his penchant for hawthorns to let him find pictures of hawthorns particularly beautiful:

No, I shall not find a painting more beautiful because the artist has painted a hawthorn in the foreground, though I know of nothing more beautiful than the hawthorn, for I wish to remain sincere and because I know that the beauty of a painting does not depend on the things represented in it. I shall not collect images of hawthorn. (*ORR* 57, *CSB* P 137).

Rashly and yet profoundly – for behind the virtuoso descriptions of hawthorns in *Du côté de chez Swann* will be Marcel's compulsive search for love, truth and beauty (albeit at first under the aegis of the aesthetic authority and knowledge of Swann). Proust also foreshadows Marcel's equivocal Venetian quest in the 1904 article:

And my admiration for Ruskin gave such an importance to the things he had made me love that they seemed to be charged with a value greater even than that of life. This was literally the case, and at a time when I believed my days to be numbered, as I left for Venice in order to be able before dying to approach, touch, and see incarnated in decaying but still-erect and rosy palaces, Ruskin's ideas on domestic architecture of the Middle Ages. (*ORR* 59, *CSB* P 139).

and he sketches in a sentence or two the whole epic of Swann, who wastes his artistic gifts for the love of Odette:

A man becomes acquainted with a woman because she may help him reach a goal other than herself. Then once he knows her, he loves her for herself and sacrifices to her without hesitation that goal which it was merely her function to help him attain. (*ORR* 58, *CSB* P 138).

Desiring a woman's superficial beauty instead of some hidden spiritual or aesthetic truth which she merely reflects is thus equated by Proust with admiring artistic form for the accidental knowledge it conveys.

Possibly reflecting some realisation that his own creative work would come to evolve quite centrally in relation to this problem, Proust's attitude to Montesquiou's idolatry mellows, and in his later tribute to Montesquiou, 'Un professeur de beauté', he sees the positive side above all, seeing in Montesquiou's as in Ruskin's erudition a superior control over memory:

This gift consists primarily in seeing clearly where others see only confusedly ... You go to the Louvre and look at a Pisanello. M. de Montesquiou then shows you, in the background of the portrait, some flowers which you might well not have noticed. And that is not the end of it ... M. de Montesquiou has already identified them as ancolia and remarked on the accuracy of their depiction ... The author's erudition enables him to refer every experience to reminiscences which most of us have not classified so carefully in our memories.   (*CSB* P 517).

And he hints in his review of the translation of *The Stones of Venice* that there can be a way to salvation through idolatry itself, through heightened artistic awareness of experience:[16]

now that we have returned from our Ruskinian pilgrimage, which was full of painstaking activity, now that we will seek truth rather than pleasure, the pleasure will be all the greater and Venice will pour forth the greater enchantment for having been for us a place of study and for offering bliss as a supplement. Our pilgrim's passion for stones which had started as thoughts and became thoughts again for us, led us to hear such admirable prayers beside the waters! To the colours of the heavens of Venice, of the mosaics of St Mark's, will be added new colours, more prestigious even because they are the very shades of a marvellous imagination, the colours of Ruskin, which in his prose, like an enchanted vessel, sail round the world! (*John Ruskin: Les pierres de Venise.* Trad. par Mme Mathilde P. Crémieux).   (*CSB* P 521–2).

Even then, of course, the erudition must be subsumed into creative artistry, for Ruskin himself can be the most tedious of idolaters, as Proust notes in his 'Journées de pèlerinage', saying that in a study of St Mark's Basilica he finds that Ruskin spends pages describing one insignificant bas-relief (*ORR* 8, *CSB* P 730).

Jean Autret has shown, however, how much of Ruskin there is to be found in *La Recherche*, particularly as regards Proust's treatment of French religious architecture.[17] I attempt, in the following pages, to identify some passages of the novel where a Ruskinian subtext is active in a Venetian context, through allusions to Ruskin's writings or to works of art mentioned by Ruskin.

With his own work on Ruskin finished, Proust was able to give free rein to his hero's own complex quest for artistic truth, and to focus it on Venice. It is generally agreed that Proust started work on *A la Recherche du Temps perdu* in about 1908, two years after his translation of Ruskin ended with the publication of *Sésame et les lys* in 1906. In the version of *Contre Sainte-Beuve* published by B. de Fallois in 1954, which appears to contain material similar to, or overlapping, the earliest drafts of the *Recherche*, the Venetian theme is dominant. It was already potently associated with memory and revival at the end of the preface to *Sésame et les lys*. In *Contre Sainte-Beuve*, critical comments and subjective anecdotes alike circle around desire for and memories of Venice, and although the quantity of text mentioning or describing Venice is not predominant, these references recur at significant psychological junctures in the guise of a refrain or a leitmotif.[18]

It is these Venetian themes and motifs, as well as Venetian works of art referred to by Proust, which I shall be considering, in relation to the structure and strategy of the *Recherche*. I believe that the internal allusions, tensions and structures created by the references to Venice and to Venetian art, are crucial to a proper understanding of the *Recherche*.

2

Desire, ideal, remembrance – the Venetian syndrome

> On construit sa vie pour une personne et, quand enfin
> on peut l'y recevoir, cette personne ne vient pas, puis
> meurt pour nous et on vit prisonnier dans ce qui n'était
> destiné qu'à elle.　　　　　　　　　　Marcel Proust

As Proust himself hesitated before the challenge offered to his desire
by the real Florence or Munich or Constantinople, and only felt
free to visit Venice when liberated from the living shadow of Ruskin,
yet needed to see Venice through the textual eyes of Ruskin, so
Marcel the child falls prey to such nervous commotion when promised a journey to Venice that he makes himself too ill to travel.
And if Venice seems to tempt the young man with an apotheosis
of artefacts and sexual opportunities, it still seems to be unattainable
as long as he lives with Albertine, since its erotic attractions would
threaten their uneasy relationship.

Whereas for Proust Venice became attractive around the turn of
the century, when as a grown man and a minor society writer he
attempted to establish a more serious reputation through his work
on Ruskin, in the case of Marcel Venice is posited as one of his
earliest symbols of artistic and sexual accomplishment and excitement. Marcel initially has an appreciation of Venice as a cultural
goal as powerful as desire; somewhat to his surprise he finds that
when he loses Gilberte, his desire to see Venice is not swept aside
by his nostalgia for her: he comes to see Venice as an alternative
pleasure (K I 682, P I 634). The rather gentle counterpoint between
sexual desire and cultural fantasy becomes more acute, and yet more
confused, when Marcel is living with Albertine. In one moment
of *vague à l'âme*, when he decides to court Andrée rather than marry
Albertine, it is not so much a question of suppressing one of the

terms (cultural fantasy, sexual fulfilment) in order to nurture the other, as a question of facing the ultimate clash between freedom and desire. If married to either Albertine or Andrée he would have to take her to Venice, which would spoil it for him (K II 1150, P II 1113).

Marcel's withdrawal from this sexual challenge is perhaps merely a heightened example of the familiar Romantic problematic inherited by Marcel, that approach towards attainment of the desired object in reality provokes withdrawal: he falls ill at the moment of leaving for Venice, he falls out of love with Albertine at any moment when marriage seems suddenly practicable – and these withdrawal symptoms are related to actual disappointments with the real Balbec and a real *Phèdre* (La Berma) which spoil his types of imaginary perfection in travel and art (K II 41, P II 45).

The polarity between culture and desire is exacerbated in *La Prisonnière* and *La Fugitive*. In these volumes Marcel's erotic adventure reaches its climax, and Venice is attained. Well before such crises, however, the links are interwoven. The desire to write, and to see Venice, is on one occasion presented casually as if equivalent to an erotic urge: 'the desire for handsome lady's-maids, and especially for Mme Putbus's, the desire to go to the country in early spring to see once again hawthorns, apple trees in blossom, storms, the desire for Venice, the desire to settle down to work' (K III 81, P III 86). Superficially the connection is only metonymic, these three desires being connected as it were only by their status as equally repressed urges. But as so often in Proust, the metonymic contagion is indicative of psychological relationships: *both* sexual relief and cultural fulfilment could be attained in Venice, and we cannot help seeing the authorial urge as somehow rooted in the libido rather than the intellect when it is narrated in this contextually determined way, and overdetermined by the wider structuring of the narrative, which inserts this musing itself within the erotic context of Marcel awaiting the return of Albertine in order to tax her with her female friendships. On another occasion the inner life of 'la petite bande' is portrayed as being as desirable as an unknown city, and the disillusionment felt once they are known, is seen as parallel (K III 168–9, P III 171).

Venice thus comes to stand for a whole universe of lost cultural and sexual opportunity, for all the unattainable and all the unknown, and Albertine's elusive sexuality becomes an insurmountable barrier to experience and knowledge: 'a treasure in exchange for which I had forfeited my freedom, my solitude, my thought' (K III 336, P III 331), so far are the erotic promises of Venice as dangerously attractive to Albertine as they are to Marcel. A similar erotic bind strangles Marcel even in Paris, where his desire to see Venetian painting in the Louvre as well as paintings by Elstir in the Luxembourg is tempered by the knowledge that their subject is lasciviously attractive to Marcel himself, and therefore too dangerous to tempt Albertine with – after all, Marcel himself knows the attractions of Parisian girls (K III 412, P III 404–5).

There is nonetheless a romantically pure side to the Venetian lure, with its 'decanted springtime' and 'virginal water' (K III 419, P III 412), yet this is powerless to override the fundamental erotic dilemma posed by Venice: at the peak of Marcel's anguished inability to reconcile love for Albertine with the dangerous liberty offered by Venice, he even loses the desire to go there, sick at heart with the deep-rooted incompatibility (K III 428, P III 422). At this nadir of frustration, when Albertine announces her departure, the emotional shock and the very possibility of accomplishing his wishes seem to numb his desire to depart (K III 431, P III 424).

And, once Albertine has left, it is she, not Venice, who becomes the forbidden and elusive goal (K III 455, P III 447). But, with a return of the pendulum worthy of Constant's fickle hero Adolphe, this recrudescence of desire brings in its wake fantasies of Venice and women – 'imaginer Venise et de belles femmes inconnues' – transferring his longing for total possession of Albertine towards the goal of possession of the erotic and cultural unknown. Marcel's uneasy conscience is shown by his need to justify these urges by equating them with Albertine's need to visit Tours and look for girlfriends (K III 483–4, P III 474).

The news of the death of Albertine only heightens the paradox: Marcel's desire for Venice is fanned as if by the Easter wind (K III 488, P III 478), and yet in her death Albertine is an even greater obstacle to enjoying Venice than she was when alive – in a magnificent image Proust compares her presence to that of a vase which both separates him from but contains the essence of the desired experience: her death breaks this vase (which we could imagine as made of Venetian glassware, in keeping with Proust's constantly associative, metonymic inspiration):

Venice, where I had thought that her company would be irksome (doubtless because I had felt in a confused way that it would be necessary to me), no longer attracted me now that Albertine was no more. Albertine had seemed to me to be an obstacle interposed between me and all other things, because she was for me their container, and it was from her alone, as from a vase, that I could receive them. Now that this vase was shattered, I no longer felt that I had the courage to grasp things, and there was not one of them from which I did not now turn away, despondent, preferring not to taste it. (K III 492, P III 483).

The theme of desire attains its apotheosis and yet is fundamentally modified when the hero at last arrives in Venice. His mother allows her love to show in almost sensual terms, as if liberated by the death of her rival, Albertine, from the need to hide it, since Marcel's indifference for the lost Albertine has perhaps not quite fortuitously coincided with his mother becoming the agent fulfilling his deepest desires by taking him to Venice. With open arms the golden angel enthroned upon the Campanile promises a purer bliss than that offered by the hero's previous angel, Albertine (K III 637/379, 389–91, P III 623/372, 383). As Marcel continues to forget her, he is able to fulfil his lust for Venetian girls, transferring to them in the process some of his past desire for Albertine, in a perfect inversion of the figure which made him desire them in opposition to her (K III 641, P III 626). At last therefore he penetrates the city of the unknown: as he wanders secretly accosting unknown girls at will, he feels that he is exploring the interior of some arcane, prohibited temple. If the Venetian seductions are partly a vicarious possession of the lost Albertine (Marcel desiring girls she would have resembled, or coveted), and a retrospective attempt to gain a fuller, more empathetic knowledge of her, through knowledge of her desires, it is nonetheless a liberation from her through erotic fulfilment which bypasses her person (K III 642–3, P III 628).

Tendentiously, the cultural image of Venice itself is distorted by the gravity of desire, as in the case of the excitingly ill-famed maid of the baronne Putbus, who is described to Marcel by Saint-Loup as being 'wildly Giorgionesque' (K II 721, P II 696), and then becomes just 'the "Giorgione"' (K II 780, P II 753). In fact the figure of desire so saturates the Venetian topos that even when comparing Venetian buildings to an exhibition of Dutch paintings Marcel sees the windows filled with girls (P III 650 [omitted by Kilmartin]), and when, transfixed by fear and lust, he contemplates a motherless Venice, drained of its poetry, and likens his vertigo before the Arsenal basin (with its sheltered waters opening out into the ambient depths of the lagoon) to the repulsion he felt as a child at the 'bains Deligny' (a famous Parisian swimming pool quite illogically afloat in the Seine), there is a strong erotic strain. The child accompanying his mother to bathe felt that in some way the 'little bedrooms' (chambrettes) of the pool were connected with some proliferating bodily promiscuity at the same time as some fathomless deep: 'one felt to be in communication with invisible depths crowded with human bodies' (K III 668, P III 653).

The panic induced by the problem of form being overrun by content (whether Venice by Albertine, a pool by the surrounding waters) alerts us in advance to the fact that both desire and place are subject to mental structuring, and create such structures.

Beyond desire, beyond culture even, Venice appears as a figure of the ideal and of memory itself. This is not new to Proust, nor was it to Ruskin. It is a typical Romantic topos, perhaps most quintessentially exemplified by Lady Morgan in her *Italy* (1821):

memory, no longer deadened by external impressions, sends forth from her "*secret cells*" a thousand fanciful recollections; and as the spires and the cupolas of Venice come forth in the lustre of the mid-day sun, and its palaces, half-veiled in the aërial tints of distance, gradually assume their superb proportions, then the dream of many a youthful vigil is realised; and scenes long gloated over in poetic or romantic pages, gradually form and incorporate, and take their local habitation among real existences – objects of delight to the dazzled eye, as once to the bewildered imagination.

(Morgan II 452, cit. Clegg 29).

Lady Morgan also notes that Venice 'even when seen . . . still appears rather a phantasm than a fact' (ibid.).

Early in *Combray* the middle-aged narrator explains how on waking in an unfamiliar bedroom his confused dreams and memories would move him back and forth in time and place, and how, before trying to get to sleep again, he would deliberately cultivate the memory of his former life in Combray, Balbec, Paris, Doncières and Venice (K I 9, P I 9). The narrator remembers Venice as one of his formative experiences, an experience which is presented as distinctly self-conscious, perhaps even archetypal of experience being refracted through the act of consciousness that both records and constitutes it.

Venice, as the type of imaginary sophistication and perfection, is opposed by the young Marcel to Françoise's naive rustic pleasure in hearing the frogs croaking at nighttime in Combray (K II 19, P II 24), yet at the same time he begins to suspect that his disappointment in Balbec will necessarily be repeated when he gets to Venice: 'in Florence or Parma or Venice my imagination could no more take the place of my eyes when I looked at the sights there' (K II 144, P II 143). And indeed, as the novel progresses Venice becomes more deviously threatened by stereotype through the familiarity of polite society with its charms. Mme de Cambremer prefers the 'little rios' to the Grand Canal and romantic sunsets (K II 841, P II 813); and Mme Verdurin sends Mme Putbus off to Venice for her holidays (K II 963, P II 923).

When Marcel does arrive in Venice the experience is neither one of destruction nor one of straightforward fulfilment of his ideal, but rather a readjustment of the shapes of ideal and of memory. The narrator defends the reality of the magnificent images of Venice recorded by great painters and rejects the facile assumption that backstreet Venice will be self-evidently more real than the Venice framed by famous Venetian works of art, which are paradoxically 'entrusted with the task of giving us our impressions of everday life' (K III 640, P III 626). Meanwhile the narrator allows the real urban tissue of Venice to create its own works of art, as when Marcel and his mother in their gondola see sunset over the palaces as if it were an artistic sunset over the mountains; the urban imitates nature, but it is an artistically arranged nature, created and controlled through architectural artifice:

> as the gondola brought us back along the Grand Canal, we watched the double line of palaces between which we passed reflect the light and angle of the sun upon their pink flanks, and alter with them, seeming not so much private habitations and historic buildings as a chain of marble cliffs at the foot of which one goes out in the evening in a boat to watch the sunset. (K III 643, P III 629).

In another symbiotic merging of the natural and the artistic, elegant ladies paying their evening calls ride up and down the Grand Canal as naturally as if it were the Bois de Boulogne – and their gondolas duly take on the appearance of carriages rocked by the prancing, horse-like Canal:

> we passed the most elegant women in the hazy evening light, almost all foreigners, who, languidly reclining against the cushions of their floating carriages, followed one another in procession, stopped in front of a palace where they had a friend to call on, sent to inquire whether she was at home, and while, as they waited for the answer, they prepared to leave a card just in case, as they would have done at the door of the Hôtel de Guermantes, turned to their guide-books to find out the period and the style of the palace, being shaken the while, as though upon the crest of a blue wave, by the wash of the glittering, swirling water, which took alarm on finding itself pent between the dancing gondola and the resounding marble. (K III 644, P III 629–30).

Not the least power of this figure derives from the disturbance of the expected poles of the animate and inanimate: the normally horse-like gondola, with its black, equine prow, becomes the creature of the normally road-like canal, which bucks and rocks in its panic.[1] The inversion of terms reaches an extreme limit of sophistication with the transformation being so overpowering that the *real* movement of the waves is treated as merely metaphorical ('as though upon the crest of a blue wave'), and this foregrounded artistic transformation becoming the activity of the visitors themselves, inspecting their hosts' dwellings as if they were on a guided tour. Indeed, the palaces appear to arrange themselves into a sequence as if to be visited in a museum, while at the same time the whole visit tends to aestheticise nature and society: 'in this Venice where the simplest social coming and going assumed at the same time the form and the charm of a visit to a museum and a trip on the sea' (K III 644, P III 630).

Whilst the terms of ideal and real, artistic and natural appear virtually inverted in the magical topography of Venice, the real force of memory seems to be reinvigorated. At the same time as the idealised artistic and/or erotic experience blocked by Albertine is liberated and transformed, the memory of Albertine herself comes surging forth. In a dramatic image inspired by the presence of the Bridge of Sighs and the Doges' prisons Marcel talks of the sudden release of the thought of Albertine from the 'piombi' of his memory (K III 654, P III 639). The prisons referred to are the 'piombi' in the Palace attic as opposed to the 'pozzi' in the damp basement, but Proust's image could also remind us of the 'leads' of Venetian windows (as may be seen in Saint Mark's Baptistry, with their little round bulls' eyes looking like portholes, or indeed, the Doge's Palace or the hotel Danieli, or the stained-glass windows of Saint-Hilaire), and thus remind us that his mother's amorously smiling face has recently been described as framed in the Arabian window of the hotel where she awaits him (K III 639, P III 625). In a similar figure, Oriane de Guermantes was 'framed' against a stained-glass window in the church of Saint-Hilaire in Combray. This 'framing' of both Albertine and of Marcel's mother will become more important thematically when Marcel enters the Baptistery in order to study Ruskin, and expresses a complex revision of his understanding of art, of his mother, of Albertine, and of his own vocation (K III 660–2, P III 645–6). I shall discuss this scene in more detail in chapter 8.

But the moment of the recurrence of the memory of Albertine is in itself significant (K III 654, P III 639). It is one of the important examples of involuntary memory in Proust's novel, perhaps neglected by critics because its trigger is linguistic rather than sensory. As Marcel ponders the financial implications of his Venetian desires, and realises that he would be hard-pressed to carry off a Venetian maiden to Paris, since he has squandered much of his fortune on Albertine, it is a sentence in his stock-broker's letter, saying 'I shall look after your credits' which reminds him immediately of the Balbec bathing-assistant who told Aimé that she used to 'look after' Albertine – '"It was I who looked after her", she had said' (K III 656, P III 641).[2]

For a moment the lock to the chest of memory is sprung and the prisoner (perhaps more a prisoner now repressed in Marcel's darkest memories than when she was literally locked up in Paris) breaks out, only to be immured again.[3] On another occasion the sight of 'an eagle accompanying one of the Apostles' at San Giorgio degli Schiavoni suddenly revives the feeling of pain he had felt when Françoise showed him that both of Albertine's rings had the same eagle motif.[4] This powerful second-degree memory (Françoise's comment had already caused Marcel to search his memory for clues to the donor's identity) is as uncontrolled as that of the 'madeleine' cake in *Du côté de chez Swann*, but, instead of bringing unexplained felicity in the wake of an ordinarily pleasurable event (drinking tea in Combray), the flashes of involuntary memory of Albertine's bathing or jewellery look forward to the flash of intuition released by tripping over a paving-stone, by the fact that their revelation is of pain, and yet still brings knowledge. These mini-resurrections of memories of Albertine lead straight away into the apparent resurrection of Albertine herself in the celebrated telegram:

My dear friend, you think me dead, forgive me, I am quite alive, I long to see you, talk about marriage, when do you return? Affectionately. Albertine.   (K III 656, P III 641).

We have already seen Marcel's mother's smile reach out towards him like an embrace now that Albertine is out of the way. Marcel's own urges are renewed rather than repeated: he himself now yearns for a kind of resurrection, a survival beyond the body, and immediately, as if by chance, Marcel is entering the Baptistery, Ruskin in hand and mother in tow, ready for a resurrectional experience (K III 660, P III 645). There are few enough direct references to Ruskin in the *Recherche*, and this is the first time we have seen the hero at work on something literary since his frustrating attempt to describe the Martinville steeples.[5] We can tell that this is not a simple repetition of Swann's monograph on Vermeer, for the imagery of baptism, of the death of the flesh and the rebirth of the spirit becomes dominant, and Marcel evokes the role of art in immortalising love of the mother, and he even relocates his memories of Albertine in an artistic rather than an erotic context (K III 660–1, P III 645–6).

Although Venice will remain a series of lifeless snapshots long afterwards in Marcel's memory (K III 897–8, P III 865), the revelation at the Guermantes' in *Le temps retrouvé* significantly resuscitates Venice (via the feeling of walking on the uneven Baptistery floor) (K III 897–900, P III 866–7). Again, it is significant that, rather than the mainly sentimental 'madeleine' incident or the largely inspirational 'steeples' writing, it should be the Baptistery sequence, with its apotheosis of hard artistic work, its consecration of the mother figure and its appeasement of eroticism, which is privileged to be reborn in Marcel.[6]

The next resuscitation, although the stiffness of a napkin ostensibly reminds Marcel of Balbec hotel napkins, uses the image of a peacock's tail to evoke the sea, and this peacock *par excellence* the bird of Fortuny's dresses and of Saint Mark's basilica, as well as of the stained-glass windows of Saint-Hilaire (K III 901, P III 868–9).

In Marcel's final reconciliation with and recuperation of the past, desire for women is also subsumed:

the slightest word that we have said, the most insignificant action that we have performed at any one epoch of our life was surrounded by, and coloured by the reflection of things which logically had no connexion with it and which later have been separated from it by our intellect which could make nothing of them for its own rational purposes, things, however, in the midst of which – here the pink reflection of the evening upon the flower-covered wall of a country restaurant, a feeling of hunger, the desire for women, the pleasure of luxury, there the blue volutes of the morning sea and, enveloped in them, phrases of music half emerging like the shoulders of water-nymphs – the simplest act or gesture remains immured as within a thousand sealed vessels, each one of them filled with things of a colour, a scent, a temperature that are absolutely different one from another.

(K III 902–3, P III 870).

Here too it is notable that the figure of Albertine is transfigured in the Baptistery at the moment of the assumption of his mother's figure in association with the mosaic iconography – just as Mary Magdalene figures alongside the Madonna beside the crucified Christ in so much Christian art.

Although Marcel tries to recapture Combray and Balbec as well as Venice, since their fleeting memories were both 'envahissants et refoulés' ('which invaded only to be driven back' [K III 908, P III 875]), it is in relation to Venice that the experience of the self is at last made whole, the links found between different visual and sexual experiences, and above all between the plastic world of perception and the inner world of desire. It is the momentary wholeness felt an instant in the Baptistery and confirmed at the Guermantes, that persuades Marcel to persist in his final decoding rather than let the experience slip away as he had after the intuitions of the Martinville steeples and the madeleine cake. Although the memories 'rose up only at once to abandon' him, somehow, for a moment, 'the past had been able to permeate' the present. It is the role of Venice and of Venetian art in mediating between these conflicting worlds of Marcel which I shall be exploring in the following chapters.

3

Some Proustian pretexts:
Titian, Racine, Vergil, Ruskin

> On devine en lisant, on crée; tout part d'une erreur
> initiale.   Marcel Proust

At certain junctures in *A la Recherche du temps perdu* a reference
to art or to literature crystallises a mood, but in so doing, it often
appears to add to the mystery and opacity of the text. In *La Fugitive*
Marcel desires a young Venetian glass-seller, and wants to take her
home to Paris, as if she were a painting by Titian (K III 655,
P III 640). The implication is deceptively simple at first sight. The
beauty of the seventeen-year-old shopgirl is enhanced by implicit
comparison to a Titian model, the erotic and aesthetic tastes of Marcel gain in nobility and plasticity. At the same time however Marcel
reveals his less ingenuous collecting urge – in the eighteenth century
gentlemen might take a *veduta* by Guardi or Canaletto as a souvenir
of their grand tour; the late nineteenth-century aesthete has the dis-
satisfying choice between the fantasy of a famous but unattainable
painting magically transferred from the Accademia to his bedroom,
and the mundane, monochrome photograph. (And on two occasions
at least Proust mocks the photographic souvenir of Venice – once
when he acknowledges in his guise of older narrator that his real
posture and scale would be that of a tiny figure in a bowler hat
surrounded by pigeons in front of St Mark's (K I 426, P I 393), and
once when he fights desperately with the obstinately fading images
of memory in an attempt to 'develop' the momentary flash of insight
afforded by tripping on a 'paving-stone', only to find that there is
nothing to view but a series of lifeless snapshots (K III 897–8,
P III 865). In fantasising the girl as a beautiful, portable painting,
he also covertly admits that the girl would be to own and occasionally
to display, to contemplate rather than consume, for decoration as

much as for company.[1] She is clearly destined to become another Albertine, a pretty butterfly transfixed, her wings a permanent display of Fortuny dresses (like the 'indoor gown [...], dark, fluffy, speckled, streaked with gold like a butterfly's wing' in which he drapes Albertine (K III 36, P III 43), or other dresses he sees in *La Prisonnière* as being a revival of the costumes painted by Carpaccio and Titian (K III 375, P III 368)). We may also remember that Albertine was likened by Marcel to Laura Dianti – who was allegedly the model for Titian's voluptuous *La Belle aux deux miroirs*, in the Louvre (K I 982, P I 920 & cf. P III 1205). This thematic recall of mutually reflecting mirrors is signalled by the occupation of the latest object of Marcel's desire – she herself purveys as souvenirs beautiful glassware including, no doubt, decorative mirrors. The seller of glass souvenirs becomes a mirror of the narrator's urge to buy her as a souvenir mirror in which to reflect his desire for Albertine, who mirrored Titian's *Belle aux deux miroirs* ... In this way the reference to the Titian painting subtly refocuses the object of Marcel's new desire (which had theoretically been liberated by the death of Albertine) as an avatar of Albertine herself.

This phenomenon is specifically identified by Marcel when he finds himself addressing the same seductive platitudes to an Austrian girl staying at his Venice hotel as he did when first attracted to Albertine (K III 663–4, P III 649). The parallel with, or rather resurgence of, Albertine is underlined by submerged allusions – Albertine was of Austrian origin (K II 1157, P II 1119); moreover, the symbol of the Hapsburg empire is the two-headed eagle, and the two rings surreptitiously acquired by Albertine, with their identical eagle motif, impose the image of the bicephalous, ambiguous eagle as the Janus-like symbol of Albertine.[2]

Even as Albertine's name is apparently ressuscitated in the over-expanded signature of Gilberte on a telegramme, so Albertine's aquiline symbolism is projected into a fixation on an Austrian girl, and her imprisonment re-enacted in fantasy through the evocation of the painting to be pinned to a wall and admired.

The problematic revival of Albertine in such figures is wittily alluded to by Marcel in a quotation from Racine's *Phèdre*, Act II scene 5. Marcel admits that he half desires to find a revivified

Albertine in these younger girls, and quotes his desire for an Albertine:

> non point telle que l'ont vue les Enfers
> mais fidèle, mais fière et même un peu farouche
>
> (K III 659, P III 644).

This (mis)quotation is treacherously apt. The original lines, spoken by Phèdre, allude to Thésée, whose attractions Phèdre finds echoed in his son Hippolyte, as if Hippolyte were a recreation of the younger Thésée. In just the same way Marcel has just admitted that, in order to relive his earlier desire for Albertine, he now desires girls of the age she was when they first met, rather than as she was when he last saw her. Phèdre's equivocal moral justification, that Hippolyte is desirable because he presents her with a pristine, attractive version of her husband, is a semi-conscious attempt to disguise the erotic source of her attraction to Hippolyte. Similarly, Marcel's disquisition on the refusal of the images of our young loves to age in phase with their fleshly originators, cloaks a simple enough compulsion to pursue eternal youth and more precisely its 'chair fraîche'. Furthermore, in loving a reflection of the young Thésée in Hippolyte, Phèdre is rejecting the real, older Thésée, just as Marcel's choice of a Venetian shopgirl or an Austrian holidaymaker show his rejection of the real Albertine in favour of younger, more vital substitutes. And indeed, the inopportune return of Thésée from Hades – news transmitted by messenger in advance of the infernal traveller's arrival – wittily echoes the telegram announcing Albertine's embarrassing return from the dead, and even turns this episode of the *Recherche* into a parody of the 'revirement' of the Racinian plot – if not a pastiche, as well as a *mise en abîme*, of the resuscitation at the heart of the plot of the *Recherche* itself.[3] Phèdre's lines imply that Thésée himself is no longer 'fidèle' or 'fier' or 'farouche', and this reminds us that Albertine is accused by Marcel of being unfaithful, unashamed and promiscuous. Racine's original verse,

> Je l'aime, non point tel que l'ont vu les enferes ...
> Mais fidèle, mais fier, et même un peu farouche,

has undergone a significant transmutation, from Racine's *tel que l'ont vu* and *fier* to Proust's *telle que l'ont vue* and *fière* (a transmutation from masculine to feminine not signalled in the text otherwise than by the transgression of the rhythm of the alexandrine). Albertine's bisexuality flickers through the shift in gender, as she takes on the colouring of a virile adventurer. And through his identification with the voice of Phèdre, Marcel becomes the older, jealous lover whose own transgressions (mirrored in the unavowed transgression of gender effected in the quotation he proffers) are ignored in the urge to possess the object of his/her desire. In addition to which, the identification with the incestuous figure of Phèdre may alert us to the fact that it is during this very Venetian sequence that the love of Marcel by his mother is suddenly unveiled – with the removal of her rival, Albertine, she herself appears liberated to the point that her smiles reach forward into the shape of an embrace:

she sent out to me, from the bottom of her heart, a love which stopped only where there was no longer any corporeal matter to sustain it, on the surface of her impassioned gaze which she brought as close to me as possible, which she tried to thrust forward to the advanced post of her lips, in a smile which seemed to be kissing me.   (K III 639–40, P III 625).

This embrace shocks maternal proprieties all the more for being released against the background of obligatory mourning for her own mother which Marcel's mother delicately circumvents:

her face shrouded in a tulle veil as heart-rending in its whiteness as her hair to me who sensed that, hiding her tears, she had pinned it to her straw hat not so much with the idea of appearing "dressed" in the eyes of the hotel staff as in order to appear to me to be less in mourning, less sad, almost consoled for the death of my grandmother.

(K III 639, P III 625).[4]

And in this context it is difficult not to recall the substitution of black for white sails carelessly perpetrated by Theseus, an oedipal gesture linked with failure to recognise filial duty and easily related to Marcel's secret philandering which makes his waiting mother white-veiled and anxious if not directly white-haired, and in her anxiety fail to recognise the returning navigator:

because, not having recognised me at first, as soon as I called to her from the gondola, she sent out to me, from the bottom of her heart, a love which stopped only where there was no longer any corporeal matter to sustain it.   (K III 639, P III 625).[5]

Proust has transposed the incest theme carefully enough. The Phaedra figure is Marcel rather than the mother;[6] the bolder love by the mother for her son (after the deaths of Albertine and of Marcel's grandmother) is interpreted as a mixture of a pious wish to celebrate the grandmother through life rather than death, and moral approval of Marcel's release from the unsuitable Albertine's clutches; the guilty wanderings of Marcel in his other guise, as the negligent Theseus, are related only obliquely to the death of the parents. In an earlier draft, the pleasures of Venice were more directly linked with the love and death of the mother. The love of the mother flowers in Venice and Marcel remembers Venice after her death as the epiphany and emblem of that love, epitomised by the oriental hotel window which framed her face:

that window has taken on in my memory the sweetness taken on by those things whose hour chimed with ours, a single hour in whose bosom we and the window were gathered together, that sunned, before-luncheon hour in Venice, that hour which somehow put us on friendly terms with it. [...] And if when later on I saw it again, I wept, it was simply because the window said to me: "I remember your mother so well".

(*BWSB* 66, *CSB* F 123).

In the published text there is no longer a real return to weep by the same window on a second trip to Venice, but a muted nostalgia on seeing an imitation of the window in a museum, and the shared intimacy of mother and son is revived through a more artistic imitation:

that window has assumed in my memory the precious quality of things that have had, simultaneously with us, side by side with us, their share in a certain hour that struck, the same for us and for them; and however full of admirable tracery its mullions may be, that illustrious window retains in my eyes the intimate aspect of a man of genius with whom we have spent a month in some holiday resort, where he has acquired a friendly regard for us; and if, ever since then, whenever I see a cast of that window in a museum, I am obliged to hold back my tears, it is simply because it says to me the thing that touches me more than anything else in the world "I remember your mother so well." (K III 640, P III 625).

And the link between erotic betrayal and incestuous passion was originally much sharper, since his mother stood as a direct alternative

to his Venetian desires, before Marcel was given the added complexity of his relationship with Albertine:[7]

The unbearable recollection of the distress I had caused her brought
back an agony that only her presence and her kiss could heal.... I felt
how impossible it would be to set out for Venice, for any place on earth,
where I should be without her.... I am no longer a happy creature, dallying
with a wish; I am only a vulnerable creature in torments of mind. I look
at Mamma. I clasp her in my arms.   (*BWSB* 67, *CSB* F 124).

Rather than such naive and forced expressions of filial passion, it
is the ironic final version, with its labyrinthine Racinian subtext,
and its artistic framing, which manages to convey the power of
subterranean desire.

The death of Swann, whose amorous and artistic activities in the
novel are so often an extrapolation of those of the protagonist, is
also connected with Venice, and with betrayal. It is introduced
through a strange allusion to Vergil, in *Le côté de Guermantes*. Swann
interrupts the social whirl of the duc and duchesse de Guermantes
to bring Oriane a photograph. One of Swann's roles in the novel
for Marcel has always been that of a purveyor of images – a coiner
of faintly blasphemous, Botticellian motifs for Odette or of Giottesque forms for the kitchen maid, a procurer of engravings of more
uplifting visions by Titian of Venice or Gozzoli of Abraham. It
is typical of Proust's contrast between Swann's protracted, brilliant
failure and Marcel's slow, subjective, opaque maturation, that Swann
should return with a Venetian trophy in the shape of a large, real
photograph instead of an imaginary Titian. After an inconclusive
attempt to revive his study of Vermeer, Swann's last work is a sadly
pedantic and tangential piece of iconographic research, connected
with Venice, but only because of the Guermantes' heraldic vanity.
Having mentioned the *Scuola San Giorgio degli Schiavoni* to the Guermantes, and its historical link with the neighbouring *Scuola San Giovanni* (more properly the *Scuola di San Zuane del Tempo*, merged
with the *Scuola San Giorgio* in 1551),[8] Swann has been told by the
Guermantes that the founders of *San Giovanni*, the Knights of
Rhodes, descended from the Knights Templar, are allegedly ancestors of the Guermantes. The ailing Swann throws his last energies

into procuring a photograph showing both sides of a coin of the Order of the Knights of St John of Malta (via Rhodes and Jerusalem), which shows a version of the Guermantes family crest (K II 596, 607–8, P II 574, 585). One immediately thinks of Marcel's later, emotive process of association, whereby 'an eagle accompanying one of the Apostles' at *San Giorgio degli Schiavoni* (which he visited only for its splendid sequence of paintings by Carpaccio) revives a poignant memory of Albertine's infidelity, symbolised by her ill-gotten pair of eagles: Swann's two-sided coin anticipates and parodies the motif, in a purely formal, passionless reflection.[9]

At all events the largeness of the photograph and the neatness of its envelope are noted by the dilettante Duchess, whose exquisite politeness matches her coquettish exploitation of Swann's extravagantly devoted gesture, whilst the Duke is exasperated by such documentary, artistic intrusion into his own interminable oral exposition of family history. In a scene which later becomes even more poignant when the news of Swann's mortal illness takes second place to the Duchess's choice of shoes to match her evening dress, Swann is rudely dismissed by the Duke while the Duchess with a more refined cruelty ekes out her own theatrically effusive interest (designed as much to annoy the Duke as to flatter Swann), until the moment when she declares her intention of using the envelope protecting the photograph as a parodic visiting card to send to the Countess Molé, to point out that the latter has flouted niceties by presenting a used envelope in lieu of a visiting card. Mme Molé's envelope/card is already 'almost twice the size of an ordinary visiting card' (K II 613, P II 590); Swann's envelope, according to the valet, is 'so large that I didn't know if I could get it through the door' (K II 612, P II 589). There is here, as well as the wittily inflationary riposte of the Duchess, a more sinister expansion of Swann's gifts of photographic reproductions to Marcel at Combray (remembered at this moment by Marcel, who is present at the scene (K II 614, P II 591)) – the size has vastly increased, the artistic value has infinitely shrunk. In a powerful *mise en abîme* the original motif has grown into an enormous, empty shell of its former structure.

Amid this tragi-comic ballet of inconsequential cross-talk, punctuated by Oriane's half-hearted efforts to get her valet to open the envelope containing the photograph without actually spoiling it (and possibly without wanting the photograph to be displayed and thus interrupt her own brilliant patter), Swann himself interrupts with an apparently academic aside: 'Extinctor draconis latrator Anubis' (K II 613, P II 591).

Oriane recognises the reference to the dragon – the *Scuola San Giorgio* is beautifully decorated with nine paintings by Carpaccio, including three on the legend of St George and the dragon – but she says that she does not understand the reference to 'latrator Anubis'. Swann does not explain. The editors of the Pléiade edition supply the appropriate reference to Vergil, *Aeneid* VIII, 698. The curious reader will find that Vergil wrote:

> Omnigenumque deum monstra et latrator Anubis
> contra Neptunum et Venerem contraque Minervam
> tela tenent,

depicting the jackal-headed 'baying Anubis' as one of the monstrous guardians of the Underworld, fighting off even the powerful Olympian gods. Swann's aside – all the more seditious for its apparently simple, coherent, self-sufficient, gnomic rhyming form, and its innocuous reference to St George – is in fact a bogus quotation, a collocation of a fragment of Vergil ('latrator Anubis') with an apparently unrelated Latin motto ('Extinctor draconis'). With Swann announcing his imminent death to a fussy Oriane who thinks that he is 'exaggerating', but wants to humour his feelings, and a Duke who is determined to ride roughshod over Swann's artistic research and the feelings of a dying man, it is no doubt the Duke who is lampooned (for the satisfaction of Swann alone, and that of the occasional reader – for there is little likelihood that the Duke will understand the allusion, although it could be construed as a direct address to him in the vocative just as well as a nominative aside in apposition to him) as 'latrator Anubis', the baying jackal patrolling the borders of death, and 'Extinctor draconis', a slayer of threatening social or artistic dragons, like some bestial St George. Moreover, one of the functions of Anubis is to convey his unfortunate guests Charon-like over into the realm of the dead, and one can thus see Swann accusing the Duke of welcoming or hastening his death.

Thus the insertion of a fragment of Vergil into Swann's discourse – without ruffling the surface of his erudite allusions – enables Proust

to deploy the thematics of death. But the reader may also recognise
the words 'Latrator Anubis' as the heading of the second chapter
of *St Mark's Rest*[10] by Ruskin. Ruskin quotes the above-mentioned
lines from Vergil in the course of the chapter (unfortunately omitting
the last two words, and thus presenting his hapless reader with a
verbless couplet with a full stop after 'Minervam'). Ruskin's argument is that St George and his dragon are a historical development
of the classical Perseus and the monster guarding Andromeda, and
that the dragon figures in Egyptian mythology as a crocodile: Ruskin's brief is partly to point a spiritual and artistic continuity between
the first patron Saint of Venice, St Theodore with his crocodile,
and Carpaccio's St George.[11] Vergil's syncretistic Underworld provides Ruskin with a nice textual mirror for this insight (Ruskin,
St Mark's Rest pp. 26–7). Swann's rejoinder becomes more complex.
With a final melancholic but erudite tag Swann has shown off both
his Ruskinian learning and the Ruskinian 'idolatry' which makes
him (and Ruskin) ultimately fail in the eyes of Proust. (Even Ruskin's
creative and informed discussions of the Carpaccio cycles of paintings dealing with St George and St Ursula are marred for the modern
reader by Ruskin's growing obsession with the base materialistic
instincts that the dragon and crocodile symbolised for him, and
with the unnerving idea that St Ursula was personally looking after
his life.) Proust in his pastiche of Ruskin (*CSB* P 201–5) shows
that he is fully and critically aware of Ruskin's tendency to allow
a proliferation of erudite allusion to divert him from the point of
his analysis. Swann's whole life is an illustration of this tendency.

The presentation of the photograph to the Guermantes, in all
the tragedy of its exhausting artistic futility, is placed by Proust
alongside, that is, just after, the exhibition of Elstir's paintings, where
Proust is able to show an example of genuine artistic creativity.
Proust's insights are often obtained by this kind of large, ironic
self-cancelling structure. But if we look at the *Phèdre* and the *Aeneid*
quotations themselves, we find a miniaturised version of the same
process. They are quotes within quotes – Marcel or Swann referring
to Racine or to Ruskin's Vergil – and both quotations develop,
at the same time as they subvert, certain insights and structures
of the surrounding text. Indeed, a considerable part of their impact
is in their subtle infiltration of the textual mass while appearing

to be less a part of its supporting structure than a decorative part of its surface. Marcel wields a familiar Racinian verse, Swann lets fall a line of Latin doggerel, which in both cases seem to form a harmless arabesque on the smooth surface of their rhetorical discourse. Yet on examination these grafted fragments of extraneous text work like pieces of grit in the oyster of Proust's text, requiring that text to form a preciously contradictory blister of sense around them in order to incorporate their recalcitrant message in its dialectic.

This process we might well compare to the process of 'incrustation' which Ruskin mentions as being the principle of the Venetian school of architecture as exemplified in the mosaic- and marble-strewn walls of St Mark's:

.the school of incrusted architecture is *the only one in which perfect and permanent chromatic decoration is possible* ... the ruling principle is the incrustation of brick with more precious materials ... the system of decoration is founded on this duplicity ... every slab of facial marble is fastened to the next by a confessed rivet and ... the joints of the armour are ... visibly and openly accommodated to the contours of the substance within ... It is at his choice either to lodge his few blocks of precious marble here and there among his masses of brick, and to cut out of the sculptured fragments such new forms as may be necessary for the observance of fixed proportions in the new building; or else to cut the coloured stone into thin pieces, of extent sufficient to face the whole surface of the walls, and to adopt a method of construction irregular enough to admit the insertion of fragmentary sculptures; rather with a view to displaying their intrinsic beauty, than of setting them to any regular service in the support of the building.

(*Stones of Venice*).[12]

A bright, simple allusion to Titian reflects another; a witty reworking of lines from *Phèdre* enriches Proust's repertoire of Racinian quotations, a fragment of Ruskin's Vergil joins the many echoes of Proust's master. These quotations are 'incrustations' of 'precious materials' in the brick of Proust's text, providing a 'chromatic' decoration in their overall scale. But they are quotations recited ironically by Proust or Marcel or by Swann, and their 'confessed rivets' are 'visibly and openly accommodated to the contours of the substance within', by Proust's signalling of their 'joints of armour': it is patent that no Titian could be bought as a souvenir; *Phèdre* has suffered a sex-change; Vergil has been sabotaged by the addition of a low-grade, ready-made rhyming fragment.

Yet Proust has 'cut out of the sculptured fragments such new forms as may be necessary for the observance of fixed proportions in the new building': the Titian image reverberates on the same wavelength as images of gilded imprisonment and sexual repetition compulsion; Racine's verse helps to integrate an enormous submerged structure of transgressional desire; Ruskin's Vergil provides an Ariadne's thread to help escape the monster Idolatry lurking at the heart of Marcel's aesthetics. Proust's 'duplicity', like that of the builders of St Mark's according to Ruskin, is intentional:[13] we must see the rivets holding on the marble, in order to appreciate that, as well as being witty in their own right, the quotations reveal subtle formal echoes of the wider textual brickwork. But where Proust's duplicity is double, in that behind the surface duplicity is a profounder duplicity yet – the apparently subversive, non-weight-supporting 'fragmentary sculptures' *are*, in a sense, the building: there appears to be no plain brickwork behind Proust's mosaic; the whole structure is formed, and underpinned, by inter-related fragments; it is all one enormous, three-dimensional mosaic.

4

'Superiore all'invidia' –
Proust's transpositions of Ruskin

Moi, c'était autre chose que j'avais à écrire, de plus long,
et pour plus d'une personne.　　　　Marcel Proust

A certain romantic view of Venice is projected by the older narrator, recreating his younger self, using terms derived from Ruskin. The references to Ruskin, generally signalled by the narrator's own use of inverted commas, have been identified by Jean Autret, by Barbara Bucknall, by Jean-Yves Tadié. David Ellison looks at the wider question of the impact of reading Ruskin on Proust's prose style.[1] I myself note a more elaborate process of subversion and transposition.

The source of Marcel's vision of Venice in *Du côté de chez Swann*, when he is promised a journey there (K I 426, P I 393), is a composite quotation from Ruskin, as follows:

Deep-hearted, majestic, terrible as the sea, the men of Venice moved in sway of power and war ... from foot to brow, all noble, walked her knights; the low bronzed gleaming of sea-rusted armour shot angrily under their blood-red mantle-folds.　　(*Modern Painters* vol. v, p. 315, 'Two Boyhoods').

the strong tide, as it runs beneath the Rialto, is reddened to this day by the reflection of the frescoes of Giorgione.　　(*Stones of Venice*, Morris p. 86).

With a poet's eye for the link between the red cloaks and the red reflection of the frescoes, Proust heightens the painterly aspect of the young Marcel's version of Ruskin, and he heightens the young man's romanticism by describing the blood-red mantles with a word which may also mean literally dripping with blood ('sanglant'):

not until then did the revelation burst upon me that on the clattering streets, reddened by the light reflected from Giorgione's frescoes, it was not, as I had continued to imagine despite so many admonitions, men "majestic and terrible as the sea, bearing armour that gleamed with bronze beneath the folds of their blood-red cloaks" who would be walking in Venice next week.   (K1426, P1393).

This should make it clear that the young Marcel is *more* romantic than Ruskin; indeed, this insight could only be reinforced by knowledge of *The Stones of Venice*, which perpetually harps back to a golden age of artistic creativity and political integrity which Ruskin sees missing from post-Renaissance, let alone nineteenth-century Venice: Proust's model of romantic idealism and actual disappointment is already the moral fabric of Ruskin's writing.

Another seemingly straightforward example of Marcel's Ruskinian yearnings repays closer scrutiny. On two occasions Marcel notes that the Titian paintings in Venice are surrounded by water, are reached via water:

I reflected that already the Ponte Vecchio was heaped high with an abundance of hyacinths and anemones, and that the spring sunshine was already tingeing the waters of the Grand Canal with so deep an azure and such noble emeralds that when they washed against the foot of a Titian painting they could vie with it in the richness of their colouring.   (K1425, P1392).

I should enjoy the same rapture as on the day when a gondola would deposit me at the foot of the Titian of the Frari or the Carpaccios of San Giorgio dei Schiavoni.   (K1475, P1440).

Since just about every painting and building in Venice could be described as water-bound, the recurrence of Titian in this context could well be due to Proust's knowledge of a passage from Ruskin's *Praeterita*, which he refers to in his preface to *La Bible d'Amiens* (*CSB* P76) (without mentioning the Titians). The original passage is an anecdote where Ruskin recounts flooding in Venice at high tide, when one could enter Danieli's hotel (frequented by both Ruskin and Proust) directly by gondola (leaving the gondola, the canal and the spectator absurdly framed inside the palaces alongside the Titians):

and then all along the canal side, actual marble walls rising out of the salt sea, with hosts of little brown crabs on them, and Titians inside.
                                           (cf. Whittick, *Ruskin's Venice*, p. 42).

The comic equation of the Titians with the crabs reduces the Titians to the status of some crustacean clinging to the walls of palace and gallery after being flung up there by the tide of history. Proust may well have remembered this comic vision and transferred to his own Titians their spurious aquatic halo, to underline the distance between Marcel's childish desire to see the Titian paintings in their location on a canal, or even Carpaccio's paintings for the same reason, and the mature interest of Elstir and the older protagonist in the historical and structural riches of Carpaccio's paintings. In fact, Titian's paintings are never quite rescued from an ironic watery framework.

The hero's first glimpse of Titian had been an engraving of one of Titian's paintings, which had the lagoon of Venice in the background (K 143–4, P 140; K III 401, P III 394). Titian not being noted for his seascapes, and Proust's critics being silent on the subject, it was a matter of some surprise to me to discover views of lagoons in two monumental Titians in the Doges' Palace – the *Doge Grimiani adoring the Faith* is kneeling smugly in a miniature Venetian seascape and the giant *St Christopher* is striding manfully over a shallowish lagoon. Due to the size of the paintings, the lagoons are actually quite large, although they are barely distinguishable in postcard- or book-size reproductions. However, Ruskin, in his description of Venetian paintings, comments on the *Doge Grimiani* picture in these terms:

The traveller who has been accustomed to deride Turner's indistinctness of touch ought to examine carefully the mode of painting the Venice in the distance at the bottom of this picture.

(cf. Whittick, *Ruskin's Venice*, p. 105).

Ruskin argues that Titian, in an otherwise pompous picture, is nonetheless in the artistry of the marine background a master of colour and impressionistic form; at the same time, he argues that Turner is no less precise a draughtsman than the great Titian. The use Proust makes of this snippet of Ruskinian opinion as early as *Combray*, in the context of the grandmother's determination to envelope reality in as many layers of art as possible (the lagoon within a painting, the painting within an engraving) takes on added significance once we realise that Titian's lagoon is a relatively tiny motif, rather than a focal landscape, and is painted in an untypical

Turneresque style, which nonetheless saves the whole painting for Ruskin. One conclusion might be that Proust was attracted by the idea of incorporating in a single image not only the dangers of idolatry (admiring in a painting of historical record and religious symbolism only an irrelevant landscape vignette; desiring to go to Venice because its lagoon was painted in a Titian masterpiece, copied by a reputable engraver and procured by the connoisseur Swann) but also a sketch of an appreciative critique of that idolatry – the critical ability to distinguish a piece of Turneresque impressionist landscape hidden amid the pomp of a Titian monstrosity. (This kind of critical ingenuity can itself in the hands of Swann or occasionally Marcel become a kind of inverted aesthetic snobbery, verging on idolatry . . .).

And the unintentional, almost mystical prefiguration and germination of Turner in Titian, like that of Fortuny in Carpaccio, is a model for the series of resurrections that punctuate the *Recherche*, and a graphic *mise en abîme* where the original structure secretes a miniature replica destined to overflow and transcend it.[2]

Given such subtle exploitations of Ruskin's visions of Venice, it would hardly be surprising if Proust's own style retained fragments of Ruskinian rhetoric. One of the most striking and apparently least well-motivated of Proust's Venetian images must be the curious, almost inexplicable picture of the shadows on the ground at St Mark's square viewed as blue flowers in the desert. I quote extensively, in order to show Proust's contrast between the shadow-forming process in Combray, and that operative in Venice:

as in Combray on Sunday mornings one had the pleasure of stepping down into a festive street, but where that street was entirely paved with sapphire-blue water [. . .] but the role played there by houses of casting a patch of shade at their feet was entrusted in Venice to palaces of porphyry and jasper, above the arched doors of which the head of a bearded god (breaking the alignment, like the knocker on a door at Combray) had the effect of darkening with its shadow, not the brownness of the earth, but the splendid blueness of the water. On the Piazza, the shadow that would have been produced at Combray by the awning over the draper's shop and the barber's pole was a carpet of little blue flowers strewn at its feet upon the desert of sun-scorched flagstones by the relief of a Renaissance façade. (K III 638, P III 623–4).

There is surely some reminiscence here of a conspicuous passage from *The Stones of Venice* ('St Mark's'):

And round the walls of the porches there are set pillars of variegated stones, jasper and porphyry, and deep-green serpentine spotted with flakes of snow, and marbles, that half refuse and half yield to the sunshine, Cleopatra-like, "their bluest veins to kiss" – the shadow, as it steals back from them, revealing line after line of azure undulation, as a receding tide leaves the waved sand.

(XIV, Tr. Ed. para. VIII).

Ruskin's play of azure and shadow evokes the azure of the sky, only to derive its blue from the stonework: Proust's shadows too are projected by jasper and porphyry, and formed by an unveiling of blue. Ruskin's 'azure undulation' transforms the marble into the nearby water, only to transgress the natural contours of the metaphor by equating the receding shadow with the (normally blue) tide, and equating the blue, sunlit stones (revealed by the tide) with the (normally yellow) sand: Proust makes his shadows into blue flowers strewn on a (yellow?) stony desert. Ruskin's very powerful transgression of the natural polarity of the metaphor creates a vision of the sculpted physicality of light, the fluidity of the watery green or sandy yellow stone, and the aqueous flux of shadow – thus the marble mass of St Mark's is infiltrated through Ruskin's use of metaphor and metonymy with its marine context. Ruskin it was whom Proust quoted describing Turner's art as being based on painting what he saw, not what he knew,[3] and Ruskin's Turner is commonly acknowledged to be one of the major figures behind Proust's Elstir, with his metaphorical transposition of land and water.[4] Small wonder then that Proust should have wished to rival one of Ruskin's great conceits in his own impressionistic description.

Logically the tracery of sculpture and statuary should cast its flowery shadows *contrasting* with the bright blue sky, but Proust has followed Ruskin in seeing the bright ground as a composite mixture of liquified stone and petrified sunlight ('sand' in Ruskin; 'désert' in Proust), and in seeing the shadow as a darker form of the surrounding water (in Ruskin the shadow, like water, washes clean the blue of the stones it uncovers; in Proust the shadow makes the blue water a darker blue, but that is still the colour of the sky and the water). Both Ruskin and Proust in fact transfer to the shadow the function of light: in Ruskin the blue is brighter after the play of the shadow, and the shadow is the azure of sky and water; in Proust the statue-shadow is seen as a reflection, and it appears to enable flowers to grow in a desert, the usual prerogative of sunshine and rainwater. The Elstirian paradigm is performed in Proust's text.

And yet with great tact Proust roots his own conceit in Marcel's concerns – the flowers could be derived from the hedgerows of Combray, as Combray is everywhere present in this vision of morning in Venice, and the desert could be derived from Marcel's beloved *Arabian Nights* which the oriental architecture of Venice helps him recall as a narrative model for his fantastic voyage through the city.[5]

And finally, the great discovery of the impressionist painters, that shadows are coloured, may be behind Proust's insistence that the streets of Combray, in light or in shadow, are yet shades of brown, and the canals of Venice, in light or in shadow, are yet shades of blue.

The most typically Proustian transformation of the Ruskinian vision is perhaps to avoid the extraneous call on Shakespeare and to insert a 'bearded god' who might well be Neptune, and who would therefore be particularly suited to casting a marine reflection.[6]

Proust's rewriting in *La Fugitive* of Combray in the marine terms of Venice is doubtless part of his overall strategy of resurrecting his hero's childhood experience through the sensory overlap of past and present. In this perspective we cannot help remembering the graphic vision of the church of St Hilaire in *Du Côté de chez Swann* as a ship sailing down the centuries:

an edifice occupying, so to speak, a four-dimensional space – the name of the fourth being Time – extending through the centuries its ancient nave, which, bay after bay, chapel after chapel, seemed to stretch across and conquer not merely a few yards of soil, but each successive epoch from which it emerged triumphant, hiding the rugged barbarities of the eleventh century in the thickness of its walls.   (K166, P161).

which image should be present in our minds when Marcel and his mother sail as it were almost right into the Baptistery of St Mark's by gondola (K III 660, P III 645).[7] The image of the church as a ship is so rooted in Christian imagery as to be a linguistic and architectural truism – the 'nave' (*la nef*) being designedly nautical. But there is no more powerful expression of the spiritual force of this imagery than Ruskin's thunderous exposition of the significance of Torcello cathedral, in *The Stones of Venice*:

in the minds of all early Christians the Church itself was most frequently symbolised under the image of a ship, of which the bishop was the pilot. Consider the force which this symbol would assume in the imaginations of men to whom the spiritual church had become an ark of refuge in the midst of a destruction hardly less terrible than that from which the wight souls were saved of old, a destruction in which the wrath of man had become as broad as the earth and as merciless as the sea, and who saw the actual and literal edifice of the Church raised up, itself like an ark in the midst of the waters ... let [the stranger] ascend to the highest tier of the stern ledges that sweep round the altar of Torcello, and then, looking as the pilot did of old along the marble ribs of the goodly temple-ship, let him repeople its veined deck with the shadows of its dead mariners, and strive to feel in himself the strength of heart that was kindled within them, when first, after the pillars of it had settled in the sand, and the roof of it had been closed against the angry sky that was still reddened by the fires of their homesteads – first, within the shelter of its knitted walls, amidst the murmur of the waste of waves and the beating of the wings of the sea-birds round the rock that was strange to them – rose that ancient hymn, in the power of their gathered voices: THE SEA IS HIS AND HE MADE IT: AND HIS HANDS PREPARED THE DRY LAND. (ed. Morris, p. 280).

Ruskin's vision of the church as a spiritual ark enabling its shipmates to survive the barbarity of the dark ages is close to Proust's, and in seeing the Church as a physical vessel travelling through time Ruskin foreshadows Proust's incorporation of time into his St Hilaire church, as its fourth dimension, and his use of St Mark's as the ultimate time capsule, his locus of resurrection of the past.[8]

Of all references to Venice, we might expect Proust's pastiche of the Goncourts' *Journal* to be least impregnated with Ruskinian matter. In *Le Temps retrouvé* Marcel reads a few pages of the *Journal*, and the discrepancy between their naturalistic observations and his own feelings and sensations convinces him that he cannot become a writer – just before he is to stumble upon the full-blown process of involuntary memory, revealed initially by the revival of the stones of St Mark's Baptistery in the stones of the Guermantes' courtyard.

But there are, interestingly, prefigurations of the Venetian revelation already lurking amidst the pretentious artistic notations of the *Journal*.[9] One of the most puzzling features of the passage is the reference to precise names – the Venetian architect Sansovino, the 'Hôtel des Ambassadeurs de Venise', the palazzo Barberino – and imprecise co-ordinates: a Sansovino well comes from 'a celebrated palazzo whose name I forget' (K III 729, P III 710), which is then remembered as the 'palazzo Barberino', (which does not actually exist, although there is in Venice a 'palazzo Barbarigo'). The story told by Verdurin to Goncourt is that Verdurin has the rim of a Sansovino well, carved with an Assumption of the Virgin, in a smoking-room whose furnishings originally came from a Venetian palazzo, possibly a palazzo 'Barberino', and the wellhead is now used in his Parisian mansion on the Quai Conti as an outsize ashtray.[10] Proust's satire here highlights Verdurin's and Goncourt's lack of moral interest in this desecration of art wrought by those who pursue its detail too materialistically, too possessively. Such goings-on were notoriously typical of Venetian art-history: during the crusades the Venetians looted granite columns and bronze horses for St Mark's square from Constantinople; in 1797 Napoleon conquered Venice, captured the horses, and brought them and many works of art home to France; in 1815, after the fall of Napoleon the horses were returned to Venice. Not only is Proust's 'Goncourt' story plausible, there is a likelihood that the plethora of imprecise information is intentionally typical of the Goncourts (the name of the palazzo forgotten, then remembered, but incorrectly): Proust deftly excuses a slip he made in a different Goncourt pastiche by arguing that 'Goncourt ... était toujours aussi inexact que méticuleux' (cf. J. Milly, *Les Pastiches de Proust*, p. 155).

But a little research would show us that Proust's example is very cleverly close to the truth. One of Sansovino's most famous wells, designed for the Mint, at St Mark's, was later dismantled and reassembled at a private palace (at the palazzo Pesaro).[11] And, as for the real palazzo Barbarigo, no less an authority than John Ruskin informs us that it had suffered much spoliation, and was: 'noticeable only as a house in which some of the best pictures of Titian were allowed to be ruined by damp, and out of which they were then sold to the Emperor of Russia' (cf. Whittick, *Ruskin's Venice*, p. 23). The trivialisation of Titian by water seems to have held an irresistible fascination for Proust!

Goncourt's breezy lack of interest in a man who was the most sublime architect of Venice and one of the giants of the Renaissance, repays attention. Sansovino designed the Zecca, the Loggia, the Libreria, the Basilica doors, the Baptistery font. Aretino in an immortal phrase said of him that he was *superiore all'invidia* – 'beyond envy'. Swann pays one of his elaborate tributes to him by likening Mme de Saint-Euverte's grooms to Sansovino's towering sculptures of Mars and Neptune on the Giants' Staircase at the Doges' Palace (K I 353, P I 324), but, in a moment of rare sentimentality, he pays Sansovino a more direct compliment, regretting the fact that he has never climbed this imitation-Sansovino staircase with Odette.[12] Sansovino, desecrated by Verdurin, admired a moment by Swann, could be said to be close to Marcel's heart: he is buried at the foot of the altar in the Baptistery, where Marcel experiences a kind of apotheosis with his mother (K III 660–1, P III 645–6).[13]

And there is an obvious precedent for Proust's choosing as the ultimate artistic desecration a piece of sacred Venetian architecture, sullied by smoke. He may well be rewriting in his own terms Ruskin's famous description of arrival in Venice, seen from afar as crowned by a plume of smoke, which he discovers to be emanating from the steeple of a church, used as a factory chimney:

> at the end of those dismal arches there rises, out of the wide water, a straggling line of low and confused brick buildings. Four or five domes, pale, and apparently at a greater distance, rise over the centre of the line; but the object which first catches the eye is a sullen cloud of black smoke brooding over the northern half of it, and which issues from the belfry of a church.
>
> It is VENICE.   (*The Stones of Venice*, ed. Morris, p. 52).

The Goncourt pastiche also contains an artistic comparison which we are obviously likely to try to relate to those made by Swann or Marcel (or by Proust and Ruskin). Goncourt says that the dome of the Institut Français is like the church of La Salute in a painting by Guardi. But the comparison is banal by virtue of its very obviousness. Where Marcel, Ruskin or Swann tend to highlight an eccentric detail of a painting (the lagoon in Titian's *Doge Grimiani*, a bystander in Mantegna's *Martydom of St James*) and make it suddenly central (as a Turneresque landscape, as Mme de Saint-Euverte's statuesque groom),[14] Goncourt spotlights the excruciatingly obvious dome of the Salute, at the centre of Guardi paintings such as *Il molo, le gondole e la Chiesa della Salute* in the Ca' d'Oro, or *La punta della dogano verso la Chiesa della Salute* in the National Gallery. Where Marcel and Swann tend to make a comparison with something apparently far removed from the world of the painting (a Bellini angel figures a sonata, a Giotto virtue a kitchen maid), Goncourt likens the large dome of a well-known French monument to the large dome of a well-known Venetian monument (K III 729, P III 710).[15]

The Verdurin/Goncourt school of art criticism is pilloried on another occasion in the *Recherche*, when the pretentious Polish sculptor Ski, anxious to turn a Verdurin evening into a Veronese painting, calls for wine and fruit and declares that 'there, against the sunset, it will be as luscious as a beautiful Veronese', (K II 971, P II 939). Monsieur Verdurin deflates his witticism with the remark that 'It would cost almost as much', but the first comment is crass enough in Proust's hierarchy of artistic sophistication, joining the Goncourt allusion to the Guardi *Salute* in its bland obviousness, likening a fashionable society reception to the fashionable society receptions which Veronese had some trouble persuading his patrons to see as religious occasions (witness the 'Last Supper' whose impact was so profane that he had to change the title to *La Cena in casa di Levi*, now in the Accademia), and in its focus on fairly evident details like raised wine glasses or red clouds at sunset (which appear in both the *Cena in casa di Levi*, and the *Nozze di Cana*, in the Louvre). There is little to choose between Verdurin's mercenary rejoinder and Ski's naively imitative and sumptuous notion of art.

We could contrast, for example, the greater sophistication of Swann in comparing his coachman Rémy to a bust of the Doge Loredan by Antonio Rizzo (K I 243, 250, P I 223, 229). The degree of avoidance of the obvious starts with the choice of a bust of Loredan much less well-known than the one by Bellini in the National Gallery.[16] The second refinement is then to select a minor part of the portrait, the cheekbones and eyebrows: eyes and mouths are universally considered to be more expressive of individual personality in persons and portraits than cheeks and brows. Thirdly, the comparison is made with an object as far removed as possible from the original, the solemn bust of a Venetian Doge being compared to the face of a Parisian coachman. But, finally, there is a grain of insight gained – the truth that facial features bridge distances, epochs, races and classes.[17] I shall indeed argue in the next chapter that in certain references to Bellini and Mantegna and Giotto, Marcel attains a higher degree of aesthetic and structural success than Swann, although he exploits the same approach to painting.

By now my patient reader may be feeling that it is time to leave the realm of the second-hand, and quit my analysis of Proust's covert Ruskinian structures with the scornful words of Bloch, dousing the enthusiastic Marcel's desire to visit Venice: 'Yes, of course, to sip iced drinks with the pretty ladies, while pretending to read the *Stones of Venighce* by Lord John Ruskin, a dreary bore, in fact one of the most tedious old prosers you could find.' (K I 794–5, P I 739). The diversion of the artistic pilgrimage into a pleasure cruise, tasting the ice-creams of Florian's or Quadri's in the company of charming young ladies, *Stones of Venice* in hand as encomium and alibi, is a fate so tempting that Bloch's parody could apply to any Proustian readers. It certainly applied to Proust himself, according to Marie Nordlinger's account of their stay in Venice. Painter even goes so far as to interpret this phrase of Bloch's as Proust's own oblique reply to some obscure critic (who hadn't actually mentioned Proust in his disparaging article). (II, 8).[18] But I myself prefer to think that Proust must have remembered (and possibly even hoped his readers might recognise ...) Ruskin's querulous epilogue to the Traveller's Edition of *The Stones of Venice*, where Ruskin, exasperated with the popular and even touristic success of his own work, describes tourists in Venice in these terms: 'They read *The Stones of Venice*, "helped always through the tedium of the business by due quantity of ices at Florian's, music by moonlight on the Grand Canal ..."' (J. Clegg (ed.), *Ruskin and Venice*, p. 128, quoting *The Stones of Venice*, Travellers' Edition, 1879–81, Chapter VI, 'Castel-Franco', pp. 164–5). Proust thus ironically places Ruskin's own later strictures on an idolatrous dependency on art-history and art-criticism within the texture of Bloch's pretentious and incorrect discourse (Bloch overcorrects his English pronunciation by making the 'i' of 'Venice' rhyme with the 'i' of 'ice', and he confers a spurious nobility on Ruskin – both errors are committed through his wish to display a superior knowledge). Thus Bloch's superficial criticism of Ruskin and his admirer is vitiated by his faulty discourse, and, at a profounder level, the substance of his critique contains Proust's own admission that Marcel will grow out of one, early, Ruskinian approach, into a later version of Ruskinism, and thus implicitly acknowledge a criticism of second-hand romanticism, as well as a criticism of the pursuit of knowledge for the sake of its authority.

In fact as *La Fugitive* progresses these Ruskinian temptations are covertly alluded to: Marcel makes notes on Ruskin in the Baptistery (K III 660, P III 645), between secret trips round the back streets picking up girls (K III 641–2, P III 628). And the 'music by moonlight on the Grand Canal' is orchestrated by Proust as the great nightmare of Marcel's Venetian crisis, torn between his mother and the delights of the flesh promised by the imminent arrival of Baroness Putbus's maid. A gondolier's insistent rendering of 'O sole mio' taunts and paralyses the lonely Marcel as his filial treachery and terrified lusts make its romantic strains increasingly intolerable (K III 667–9, P III 652–4).

Turner is prematurely reborn within Titian; Combray reflowers in the shadow of Venice; a church sails safely through the Dark Ages to the quayside of St Mark's; a Sansovino Virgin ascends through the smokescreen of the Goncourts' *Journal*. And just as the voice of Ruskin rises in the speech of Bloch to mock his accents, on each of these occasions an image or idea, a phrase or a vision of Ruskin is miraculously transposed into the texture of Proust's *Recherche*. Proust's attitude is neither adulatory nor derisory: he has so imbibed Ruskinian structures that Ruskin's text has become 'superiore all'invidia'.

5

Into the abyss: Bellini,
Mantegna, Giotto

> It is better for me not to stay in Italy, but to go home
> quietly and write down what I have got – else I should
> learn too much, and get nothing said.   John Ruskin

Proust's incrustation of quotation within quotation, of text within text, of image within image, the ironic adhesion of the narrator's thought to the deep structure rather than to the surface grammar of the artist cited, is particularly striking in his allusions to painting.

In Combray Proust refers to a painting by Gentile Bellini in the Accademia in Venice, *Procession in St Mark's Square*, as an image of the work of spontaneous memory, and its creative power:

But in my dreams of Combray (like those architects, pupils of Viollet-le-Duc, who, fancying that they can detect, beneath a Renaissance rood-screen and an eighteenth-century altar, traces of a Romanesque choir, restore the whole church to the state in which it must have been in the twelfth century) I leave not a stone of the modern edifice standing, but pierce through it and "restore" the Rue des Perchamps. And for such reconstruction memory furnishes me with more detailed guidance than is generally at the disposal of restorers: the pictures which it has preserved – perhaps the last surviving in the world today, and soon to follow the rest into oblivion – of what Combray looked like in my childhood days; pictures which, because it was the old Combray that traced their outlines upon my mind before it vanished, are as moving – if I may compare a humble landscape with those glorious works, reproductions of which my grandmother was so fond of bestowing on me – as those old engravings of the *Last Supper* or that painting by Gentile Bellini, in which one sees, in a state in which they no longer exist, the masterpiece of Leonardo and the portico of Saint Mark's.

(K I 181, P I 165–6)

Gentile Bellini's painting is thus referred to as a painting which

1   Gentile Bellini. *Procession in St Mark's Square*, Accademia, Venice.

shows St Mark's before the major alterations of the seventeenth century. Ruskin had made the same observation.[1] The mosaics of St Mark's preserved in the Bellini painting, or the *Last Supper* of Leonardo preserved in an engraving, preserve and resuscitate buildings long since disappeared, as Marcel's daydreams revive the vanished Combray. But the painting is anything but a simple mnemonic document.

It shows a procession passing before the intricately decorated façade of St Mark's, with its bronze horses and its thirteenth-century mosaics. The mosaic over the south-west door is the one that remained to be admired by Ruskin, and the one that remains today. This mosaic portrays a procession passing before the intricately

decorated façade of St Mark's, with its bronze horses and its ...
but here the regression becomes theoretical, as the mosaics *en abîme*
are too small (both in Bellini's painting and in the actual mosaics
at St Mark's) to be represented by more than perfunctory arabesques,
a few decorative twirls, a purely formal gesture, an elegant signature
by the artist, acknowledging the existence in principle of the infinite
regression, impossible to attain in practice, but formulated in the
mise en abîme of Proust's text. For the experience referred to within
this metaphorical development is that of the childhood memory of
Combray, itself generally a dim landscape, but here and there preserved beyond its natural demise by an image graven in Marcel's
fantasy. The patch of bright experience shining out from the faded
canvas of memory is likened, within the framework of a major comparison of memory to the preservation of lost architecture in painting
– and even this comparison is as it were encapsulated by the reference
to the preservation of painting itself in engraving – to the elusive
landscapes distanced yet preserved in the grandmother's engravings
of Leonardo and Titian (which included an engraving of Leonardo's
Last Supper . . .) (K I 43–4, P I 40). The vertiginous spiral of Proust's
metaphor presents the very *substance* of the Combray memory (the
grandmother's artistic prejudice) as the spiral mental *structure* ensur-
ing its own perpetuation, through transformation into a more lasting
aesthetic form: the Bellini painting resuscitates and fixes the mosaics
of St Mark's through its artistry as the Guermantes' paving stones
will later resuscitate the flagstones of St Mark's in Marcel's memory,
but, above all, this mental structure is already literally enacted
through Proust's metaphor itself. The figure of the self-inclusive
Bellini imagery dramatises this whole experience, suggesting the
transformational potential of mnemonic rhetoric.

Neither Proust nor Ruskin could conceivably have committed the
artistic sin of classifying the sublime angel musicians of Giovanni
Bellini as the work of his bother Gentile. For it is Giovanni's angels
who are the object of another Proustian transformation.[2]

One of Proust's earliest references to Bellini's angels would seem
to be in a note to his preface to the *Bible d'Amiens*. Proust notes
Ruskin's comment on the immaturity of Della Robbia's or Bernar-

dino Luini's angels, compared to those of Bellini in the Frari and San Zaccaria churches. Ruskin insists on the value of calm even in art conveying rapture: 'No action takes place except that the little angels are playing on musical instruments, but with uninterrupted and effortless gesture, as in a dream. A choir of singing angels by La Robbia or Donatello would be intent on their music or eagerly rapturous in it as in temporary exertion: in the little choir by Luini [...] we even feel by their dutiful anxiety that there might be danger of a false note if they were less attentive. But Bellini's angels, even the youngest, sing as calmly as the Fates weave'.[3] Proust records the key paradoxes in translation: 'attentifs à ce qu'ils chantent, ou même transportés' ... 'pleins d'une conscience craintive' (*CSB* P 81).

In *A l'ombre des jeunes filles en fleurs* the voices of Albertine and her band are likened to the instruments played by angel musicians:

And on this more varied instrument they played with their lips, with all the application and the ardour of Bellini's little angel musicians, qualities which also are an exclusive appanage of youth. Later on these girls would lose that note of enthusiastic conviction. (K I 969–70, P I 908).

The narrator has just written that women have a less flexible vocal tonality than girls, so that it is in key for him to see the assiduity and enthusiasm of Bellini's angels as specifically childish. Proust's epithets 'application', 'ardour' and 'enthusiastic conviction' are very like Ruskin's 'attentive' and 'rapture' (referring, it is true, to Della Robbian angels). Proust must have remembered his previous translation of Ruskin's rather nice oxymoron. But anyone who has seen, for instance, the Bellini *Triptych* in Santa Maria Gloriosa dei Frari, hanging in the sacristy alongside Titian's great *Assumption of the Virgin* (familiarly referred to by Proust as 'the Titian of the Frari'), or Bellini's *Pala di San Giobbe* in the Accademia (Ruskin's favourite Bellini),[4] will immediately recognise the aptness of Proust's adjectives. 'Application' is a word often applied to the strenuously well-intentioned but slightly exaggerated efforts of the practising child rather than the more straightforwardly professional adult alertness implied by 'attentive'. 'Ardour' and 'enthusiastic conviction' are slightly naive, deliberately less transcendental than 'rapture', capturing the tone of Ruskin's 'eagerly rapturous' and 'dutiful anxiety' for it is not incompatible with a certain self-conscious desire to play well and to be seen to play well. The finest variation on Ruskin's vocabulary has provided Proust with a sharp psychological insight into Bellini's portraiture.

Proust's dual metaphor superficially compares the vocalising of Albertine and her friends to the efforts of these apprentice angels, with the conceptual link, as so often in Proust's imagery, provided by metonymy – here the visual and kinetic similarity of the movements of their lips to those required when playing a wind instrument is added to the auditory similarity of the chanting voice to the musical instrument, so that the overall impression is that of the voice and lips played as a musical instrument. At the same time, the metonymic motivation of the imagery invites us to visualise the girls as a composite picture of all that is attractively girlish in Bellini's Venetian angels – the rapt, stylised sweetness of the almost carnal children in the Frari *Triptych*; the slightly awkward self-consciousness and precarious poise of the girls in the Accademia *Pala*, their eyes travelling busily while their bodies execute the music in a faultless, familiar ritual; the faintly arrogant suavity and sophistication of the rather unserious young ladies in the *Madonna del Doge Barbarigo* in San Pietro Martire in Murano; the totally human young woman, the very incarnation of female grace, curving gently over her viol in San Zaccaria, as if forming the figure of a pietà.[5]

On another occasion a Bellini angel is mentioned by Proust as the epitome of beauty. In a vertiginously complex conceit, Proust likens the *difference* between Vinteuil's sonata and his septet, to the *difference* between 'a grave and gentle Bellini seraph strumming a theorbo' and 'some scarlet-clad Mantegna archangel sounding a buccina' (K III 262, P III 260).

The terms of the comparison have their separate merits, the sonata with its simple lyrical theme being compared to the angel playing the theorbo (a kind of twin-handled lute used to accompany the human voice), with its implication of a single vocal line and a simple, accompanying melody; the septet being compared to the grander archangel playing the more sonorous buccina, which is usually the kind of ceremonial trumpet that would be played in an ensemble as a basso continuo. But within this grid there is a metonymic glide from the scarlet clothing of the archangel to the synaesthetic impression of the scarlet-sounding trumpet, and also the suggestive tension

2   Giovanni Bellini. *San Giobbe altarpiece*, Accademia, Venice.

established between the symbolic or pictorial connotations of terrestrial Bellini angels and heavenbound Mantegna archangels. Although we have to reveal a Proustian anachronism, in that no Bellini angel could play a theorbo, for Giovanni died at the beginning of the sixteenth century and the theorbo was invented towards the end of the sixteenth century, nevertheless this twin-handled lute was a nice idea of Proust's, the one set of strings working in simple harmony with the other set, as it executes the vocal accompaniment. Mantegna archangels playing buccinas are also in short supply. Mantegna's martial, triumphal trumpets may be seen for instance in the *Triumph of Caesar* at Hampton Court, but the only archangels obviously wielding trumpets are on the *Assumption of the Virgin* altarpiece of the Cappella Ovetari in the Chiesa Eremitani in Padua (conveniently situated beside the Scrovegni chapel with its Giotto frescoes familiar to Swann).

There is also the comparison between music and painting, which enables us to picture the works of a fictional composer by transposing into tonal terms the complex psychological overtones setting Bellini's fleshly girls against Mantegna's ethereal women (neither Bellini nor Mantegna appeared to entertain any doubts as to the sex of their angels ...); Bellini's chamber orchestra against Mantegna's mythical cohorts (the buccina had been used by the Roman army, and also by assorted gods and sprites of the winds and waves); the psychological insight of Bellini's portraiture against the statuesque symbolism of Mantegna (alluded to in Swann's comparisons, cf. K I 352–3, P I 324);[6] the plastic pattern afforded by contrasting the vertical thrust of the Paduan archangels and the soaring trumpets prolonging their ascension, with the discreet curves of the flesh and the elegant angles of the limbs in Bellini (a symphony of adolescent knees and elbows); Bellini's muted chromatics against Mantegna's brazen scarlet suggesting the sublime contemplation of art opposing the active process of its creation.

Mantegna provides Proust with a range of different approaches, apart from Swann's homely comparisons[7] and the synaesthetic dual metaphor just mentioned. The narrator himself is not above likening a character to a Mantegna sketch, in terms very similar to those employed by Swann (K III 981, P III 938),[8] but his own predilection

for a more sophisticated kind of anachronism, based on informed
and sensitive insight into the artist's composition, is highlighted
by Albertine's comment on Mantegna's *San Sebastiano*, that its background is a 'ville en amphithéâtre' ('a terraced city') resembling the
Trocadéro.[9] Here Proust's own mirroring structures are displayed.
Albertine perceives the architectural background of the painting in
terms of foreground (the 'ville' suggesting the importance of the
architectural detail, the 'amphithéâtre' suggesting theatrical display
as well as the more obvious (semi-)circularity of the arena and of
Proust's motif (K III 165, P III 168)). At the same time, in a process
used by Proust in many of his incrusted images, she suggests that
the extravagantly modern Trocadéro, with its 'giraffe-neck towers',[10]
has an affinity with the kind of classical architectural detail observed
by Mantegna: reminding us that the Trocadéro's chance resemblance
to the charterhouse of Pavia which Albertine also notices signals
a deeper truth – modern styles often revive ancient form; Mantegna's
and others' Renaissance painting and sculpture and architecture
revived the art of antiquity. At all events, Marcel's praise of Albertine's anachronism shows his appreciation of this kind of structural
distortion – which is close enough, after all, to the embedding of
a Turner lagoon in a Titian painting.

However, in *A l'ombre des jeunes filles en fleurs*, Marcel/Proust
himself is careful to work into his text a figure which is more fully
the stylistic accomplishment of his own theoretical position. From
Swann's relatively trivial personification and Albertine's apter identification of motif, there is a hierarchy of complexity, culminating
in the narrator's synaesthetic cross-references between pictorial and
musical structure, and then finally the virtuoso construction whereby he compares his departure to Balbec by train to an erection of
the cross by Mantegna. Here again the fragments and variants of
the San Zeno altarpiece in Verona come to mind and must have
been in Proust's mind (cf. n. 8 & 9, p. 162). One part of the *Predella*
is in the Musée des Beaux Arts in Tours – a dramatic *preghiera
nell'orto*, while the crucifixion itself from the *Pala* is in the Louvre.
Another version of the *preghiera nell'orto* is in the National Gallery
in London. The vision of these dramatic skies (there are particularly
threatening clouds in the National Gallery version) is likened by
Proust to the sight of engines belching steam up against the glass
dome of the Gare St Lazare, as the boy leaves home for the seaside:

We must abandon all hope of going home to sleep in our own bed, once we have decided to penetrate into the pestiferous cavern through which we gain access to the mystery, into one of those vast, glass-roofed 'ateliers', like that of Saint-Lazare into which I went to find the train for Balbec, and which extended over the eviscerated city one of those bleak and bound-less skies, heavy with an accumulation of dramatic menace, like certain skies painted with an almost Parisian modernity by Mantegna or Veronese, beneath which only some terrible and solemn act could be in process, such as a departure by train or the erection of the Cross.   (K I 694, P I 645).

In the first instance this image may appear to trivialise. The lowering heavens in Mantegna's paintings symbolise the cosmic tragedy of the crucifixion – in Proust's pastiche (as one might call his elaborately bathetic repetition of the Mantegna imagery), the steam clouds of the railway station express the chagrin of saying goodbye. Even at this level the pastiche reveals deeper truths – the subjective judge-ment that leaving a friend or relation can be a station of the cross in our lives, the impact of the intemperate hiss of the locomotive being a callous rebuff to feeling and a gross expression of it, the impression that the hostile wastes of the absurdly tall cupolas of the nineteenth-century railway station are both an imitation heaven and an anguishing void deserted by God. But the link of the station with painting is caught in a returning spiral – these steam clouds against their glass cloche (painted of course by a Turner and a Monet) are likened in their turn to some painting in the studio of Proust's composite impressionist painter, Elstir (the station is an 'atelier' – meaning both 'workshop' and 'studio' – the steam clouds themselves are an artificial product (steam) imitating nature (clouds) even before the art of a Monet or an Elstir comes to imitate their nature ...). Proust's text works from a vision, of steam clouds in a railway station, embeds this image within the capsule of an artistically constructed emotional equivalent (the conventional landscape of religious pas-sion haunting a Mantegna crucifixion), but then embeds this image in its turn within a larger metaphor, returning the Renaissance pas-sion to the status of a mere variant of the contemporary landscape metamorphosed by art (the dome of the Gare St Lazare caught by the contemporary artist as the modern equivalent of a crucifixion, helped by the allusion, through 'Lazarus', to resurrection). And Mantegna disappears leaving his lowering clouds, and perhaps the framework of his Cross to provide the framework of the painter's studio as it reconstructs the vault of the station in order to embed its expressive clouds ... And still behind these facing mirrors is glimpsed the major organisational structure of Proust's metaphor itself, his own textual mirror eliding steam and clouds, gilded frame and iron girders, canvas and glass, traveller, artist and martyr, writing Elstir's painting of modern passion into a controlled textual frame where it engulfs the Mantegna painting as this enclosed the religious experience of suffering.

And the inscription of this model of the infernal abyss in a model of writing is reasserted by the subtle recall of Dante (through the reference to 'abandon all hope' and 'penetrate into the pestiferous cavern through which we gain access to the mystery');[11] Dante, whose hell was an inverted conical vault full of terrible vapours and spiralling one-way tracks.

Thus we realise suddenly the simple, awesome power of Proust's figurative abyss – he has written out the structuring agony of the artist in his studio as well as the description of the beauty and the anguish of a fragment of modern life, in addition to its tendency to take on significance only within an aesthetic process, constructing its own form, through metaphoric involution.

The narrator's propensity to exploit artistic allusions as models of his own self-conscious artistry is once again contrasted with Swann's more sterile aesthetic wit in the case of Giotto.

Swann sees that the figure of Charity (from the frieze beneath the frescoes in the Scrovegni chapel in Padua), in her Empire dress, appears pregnant: whence an identification with the pregnant kitchen maid at Combray. This is clever enough of Swann, to notice that one of Giotto's cardinal virtues is in the family way. But I am not sure that critics have noted the clear distinction between this appreciation and the insight of Marcel, commenting in his adult capacity, projecting a whole network of significance back on to Giotto's Charity from the starting point of the kitchen maid: Charity appears to be standing on sacks in order to reach up to pass a corkscrew through the kitchen skylight, rather than passing her burning heart up to God as she tramples on her earthly possessions (K I 87,

P I 81). The flowers on her headband and basket are reminiscent of the kitchen maid's bunch of asparagus (K I 131, P I 121). Marcel ironically contrasts the 'virtue' of Françoise – her fine cooking – with her vicious tormenting of the 'Vertue de Padoue', the hapless fallen girl who is forced to peel asparagus despite its ill effect on her morning sickness (K I 135, P I 124). This clash between real and apparent virtue and vice is made the subject of Proust's theoretical argument. Charity is realistically portrayed by Giotto, as if unaware personally of the symbolic nature of her actions; thus too, the kitchen maid appears unaware of the 'additional symbol' of the 'ordinary ... burden' of her 'mysterious basket', however pregnant with meaning it is for others (K I 87, P I 80–1) Giotto's Charity and Justice have hard, grey features belying their noble message – and Proust finds this symptomatic of other harshly pious female representatives of Christian virtue (K I 89, P I 82).

Marcel, the young man, as far as one can thus separate him from the older narrator, is most like Swann when infatuated with Albertine, whose 'diabolo' is likened to an idol held by Giotto's Idolatry [*sic*: actually entitled Infidelity] (K I 947, P I 886–7), and most creative when referring to his own mental processes rather than to the object of his desire: he likens his own fantasies woven around the two syllables of Florence to the kind of dual perspective existing in a Giotto fresco, with consecutive actions pictured simultaneously on two separate architectural planes (K I 423, P I 389–90).[12]

The difference between Swann's and the narrator's appreciation of art is made most clear when Marcel takes a day trip from Venice to Padua and is able to see for himself the Giotto frescoes so often referred to by Swann. The frieze of vices and virtues, of which Swann had given him reproductions, is passed over in silence, and it is the roof, and the angels in the background of one of the frescoes, which catch his eye (K III 663, P III 648). There is a strikingly beautiful description of the way in which the startling blueness of the chapel ceiling (deliberately painted sky blue with gold stars by Giotto in imitation of the heavens) makes Marcel feel that the sky has moved into the chapel with him:

I entered the Giotto chapel, the entire ceiling of which and the background of the frescoes are so blue that it seems as though the radiant daylight has crossed the threshold with the human visitor in order to give its pure sky a momentary breather in the coolness and shade, a sky merely of a slightly deeper blue now that it is rid of the glitter of the sunlight.

(K III 663, P III 648).

Here Marcel splendidly echoes the intentions of the artist – Swann does not have the same kind of empathy with the artist in his own references; on the contrary, his pregnant kitchen maid seen as Charity gains her impact from the disparity between the artist's original figure and the role played by her double. Marcel also makes a witty comparison of Giotto's angels to some extinct race of fowl or to the new-born race of aviators. As with his earlier comment on the ignorance of the figures symbolising vice and virtue as to their symbolic significance, Marcel goes beyond Swann's identifications and examines the way in which the angels are as real as Envy and Charity. Instead of impersonating their symbolic message they are busily absorbed in the mechanics of flying. Proust has brilliantly noted Giotto's realism: the zooming, and looping, diving, gliding and flapping of his angels show that symbolism does not have to entail psychologism:

Constantly flitting about above the saints whenever the latter walk abroad, these little beings, since they are real creatures with a genuine power of flight, can be seen soaring upwards, describing curves, "looping the loop," diving earthwards head first, with the aid of wings which enable them to support themselves in positions that defy the laws of gravity, and are far more reminiscent of an extinct species of bird, or of young pupils of Garros practising gliding, than of the angels of the Renaissance and later periods whose wings have become no more than emblems and whose deportment is generally the same as that of heavenly beings who are not winged.

(K III 663, P III 648–9).

But it is Giotto's Envy who reserves for us the most significant lesson. When seen in reproduction, in 'Combray', Envy is noted for the realistic treatment of her symbol – her serpent's tongue is so invasive that she is totally preoccupied (in Proust's terms, like a child blowing up a balloon, a victim of a tumour of the tongue, or a patient with a spatula in her mouth), and she has no time for envious thoughts (K I 87–8, P I 81–2). But when the maturing protagonist turns his attention to his inner mental processes, in *Le côté de Guermantes*, Giotto's Envy is introduced more naturally and profoundly.

Proust examines the paradoxical state of consciousness where thought, subsisting in a dream, thinks it has dreamt its own presence, as in Dante's dream of *Inferno* XXX (see my chapter 8):

Before going to sleep, I devoted so much time to thinking that I should be unable to do so that even after I was asleep a little of my thought remained. It was no more than a glimmer in the almost total darkness, but it was enough to cast a reflexion in my sleep, first of the idea that I could not sleep, and then, a reflexion of this reflexion, that it was in my sleep that I had had the idea that I was not asleep, then, by a further refraction, my awakening ... to a fresh doze in which I was trying to tell some friends who had come into my room that, a moment earlier, when I was asleep, I had imagined that I was not asleep.   (K II 147, P II 145).

This masterly exploration of the self-reflexive dream-thought is specifically related to Venice:

Similarly, in later years, in Venice, long after the sun had set, when it seemed to be quite dark, I have seen, thanks to the echo, itself imperceptible, of a last note of light held indefinitely on the surface of the canals as though by the effect of some optical pedal, the reflexions of the palaces unfolding as though for ever and ever in a darker velvet on the crepuscular greyness of the water.   (K II 147, P II 146).

The transposition of light into terms of sound (the 'echo' of light), the effort of the mind holding on to that sense-impression translated into terms of a musical performance (the 'note' of the light 'held' on a 'pedal'), are brilliantly related, through their synaesthetic form, to the process of waking consciousness being transformed into rêverie by what Freud called the dream work. The infinitely repeated reflection of the 'palaces unfolding as if for ever and ever' provides a sumptuous plastic equivalent of the earlier exposition of the dream thought itself ('reflection of this reflection'), as well as being the perfect plastic illustration of the literal mirroring of the conceptual *mise en abîme*. And finally, the monochrome concerto of black reflected in dark grey magnificently reproduces the darkness of night and of the mind in which this cerebral passion proceeds, as well as giving a textual performance of the close interpenetration of the two shades of consciousness.

INVIDIA

3   Giotto. *Envy*, Cappella degli Scrovegni, Padua.

In the dream itself, an archetypal Proustian 'dream' in another sense is enacted: as in Elstir's paintings, the forms and substances of matter become interchanged – life becomes art through a generalised process of metaphorical exchange; partly of temporal and spatial, partly of past and present:

One of my dreams was the synthesis of what my imagination had often sought to depict, in my waking hours, of a certain seagirt place and its mediaeval past. In my sleep I saw a gothic city rising from a sea whose waves were stilled as in a stained-glass window. [...] This dream in which nature had learned from art, in which the sea had turned Gothic, this dream in which I longed to attain, in which I believed that I was attaining to the impossible, was one that I felt I had often dreamed before.

(K II 147–8, P II 146).

The dream uniting separated states of time, metaphor uniting separated states of reality – these are two themes which will only become articulated as an explicit theory of narration for Marcel much later in the novel. The dream union of an 'oriental church' with 'fourteenth-century' houses, the stained-glass window subsuming the gothic city within its waves of colour, returns the reader surreptitiously to the magic lantern and to the church of St Hilaire, which already prefigured the preservation of a medieval past in artistic form, and at the same time showed its links with a living and changing present. And the image of the gothic city enclosed by sea and set within stained-glass evoked Venice as an idealised reconstruction of time and space through art.

And yet, just as the experience of St Mark's flagstones is not realised in all its significance until revived by the stones at the Guermantes, so this dream for the time being remains a dream, rather than an understanding that the artist's way will lie along an inner path, that of subjective, pre-conscious experience. The dream is experienced as anguish rather than elation:

as soon as I tried to speak to these friends I felt the words stick in my throat, for we do not speak distinctly in our sleep; I wanted to go to them, and I could not move my limbs, for we do not walk when we are asleep either; and, suddenly, I was ashamed to be seen by them, for we sleep without our clothes. So, my eyes blinded, my lips sealed, my limbs fettered, my body naked, the image of sleep which my sleep itself projected had the appearance of those great allegorical figures (in one of which Giotto

has portrayed Envy with a serpent in her mouth) of which Swann had
given me photographs.   (K II 148, P II 146).

Yet the anguish of the narrative is belied by the sophistication of
its form. The struggling dreamer, with paralysed legs, fading sight
and speechless tongue subtly reminds us of Swann's tangential
exploitation of Giotto's vices and virtues. Proust at one stage had
planned to call a section of his narrative: 'Les Vices et les vertus
de Padoue et de Combray'.[13] Not only is Giotto's Envy a splendid
figure of Proust's suffering dreamer (dressed in nightshirt and night-
cap; groping her way forward unsteadily with one outstretched
hand, but apparently motionless with fire consuming her legs; ears
monstrously oversized as if to emphasise her passive dependence
on listening rather than on using her useless eyes: the eyes being
attacked directly by the serpent issuing forth from her mouth), her
dilemma is specifically his – that the tongue itself has become so
inflated that it fills the mouth and face to the point where she can
see nothing but her own desires, just as, for the dreamer, the dream
narrative swells and fills consciousness to the point where it produces
its own false consciousness. Now the whole agony of divided consciousness appears in this reference to Giotto – the alienation of
the dreamer from his own consciousness ('the image of sleep which
my sleep itself projected'), the inability of the dream narrative to
represent without distortion (for the peaceful void, silence, immobility and nakedness of sleep assume nightmare proportions where
the speaker/viewer/actor is blinded, gagged, bound and stripped).
Yet this arises from the perverse attempt of consciousness to fight
its dream-visions and try to translate dream-experience into terms
of representational reality, which is an exact enactment of the narrator's false quest for an authorial vocation, false because he attempts
to reproduce a reality consciously analysed by the waking mind
rather than project a subjective, inner experience. And it is envy
– of writers like Bergotte and artists like Elstir – which has blinded
Marcel into a perverse attempt to emulate them rather than develop
his own thoughts and feelings. The serpent biting its own tail
(adopted overtly by Valéry as his motto for the circularity of consciousness) is a traditional motif for the vicious circle; in this case

the vicious spiral, or *mise en abîme*, of consciousness distorting, in trying to reflect, consciousness.

Proust's novel started with the privileged consciousness of the dreamer, who: 'has in a circle round him the chain of the hours, the sequence of the years, the order of the heavenly bodies' (K I 5, P I 5). In figuring his protagonist's Venetian dream as Giotto's Envy, Proust reworks the dilemma, and the solution to the dilemma, in a form not yet accessible to the waking narrator, but nonetheless alerts the watchful reader to the eventual recuperation of experience from behind the screen that the protagonist's consciousness was erecting to view it upon.[14]

The self-reflexive dream thought, and its relationship with creativity as well as reality, is in fact explored even more acutely when the protagonist is in Venice. As the dream thought had been taken for reality, and had itself assumed as much reality as waking consciousness, in *Le Côté de Guermantes* (K II 147–8, P II 145–6), so now in *La Fugitive* reality itself appears to dissolve into fantasy, and waking consciousness turning its doubting gaze on its own memory, is tempted to dismiss it as dream (K III 665–6, P III 650–1).

The waking exploration of Venice is one of the rare experiences which bring Marcel genuinely unknown experience (as well as all the *déjà-vu* which will provide the substance and methodology of resurrection): 'It was very seldom that, in the course of my wanderings, I did not come across some strange and spacious *piazza* of which no guidebook, no tourist had ever told me' (K III 665, P III 650). In this unchartable, labyrinthine city, Marcel's mind is freed from its preconceptions, and thus too topology and matter themselves seem able to expand beyond realistic limits and contain the fantastic:

I had plunged into a network of little alleys, or *calli*, packed tightly together and dissecting in all directions with their furrows a chunk of Venice carved out between a canal and the lagoon, as if it had crystallised in accordance with these innumerable, tenuous and minute patterns. Suddenly, at the end of one of these alleys, it seemed as though a distension had occurred in the crystallised matter. A vast and splendid *campo* of which, in this network of little streets, I should never have guessed the scale, or even found room for it, spread out before me surrounded by charming palaces silvery in the moonlight.   (K III 665, P III 650–1).

This clear hint that reality is a subjective projection, secreted by the unconscious, is not yet assimilated by Marcel, who attempts to re-enact the moonlight vision by daylight in order to reinsert it into the safe order of the known and the palpable; and on failing to reconcile the two orders of perception, the nocturnal and diurnal, he concludes that the memory of nocturnal perception is an unreliable, or at least an unverifiable, fiction of sleep:

> The next day, I set out in quest of my beautiful nocturnal *piazza*, following *calle* after *calle* which were exactly like one another and refused to give me the smallest piece of information, except such as would lead me further astray. [...] And as there is no great difference between the memory of a dream and the memory of a reality, I finally wondered whether it was not during my sleep that there had occurred, in a dark patch of Venetian crystallisation, that strange mirage which offered a vast *piazza* surrounded by romantic palaces to the meditative eye of the moon.
>
> (K III 665–6, P III 651).

The composition of the vision itself has its part of metonymy (Venetian glassware providing the crystal motif, the Grand Canal introducing the 'flottement' of consciousness, but the glass and the water themselves have a more strongly reflexive and structuring function – the glass and the water (as in many Symbolist poems) indicate the devious resistance of consciousness to penetration by its own gaze: the mechanical rejection of the image by the mirror, the multiple fragmentation and refraction of glassware, the drowning of analysis and perception in the glaucous fluid of their own subjective, oneiric imagery ('I found myself suddenly brought back to the Grand Canal'), all suggest such a reading.

The Venetian glass and the beautiful palaces also suggest the presence of artistry, the insertion of a surprising and structured image of the thinker's consciousness suddenly facing him in the centre of a network of observation introduces the *mise en abîme*, and the hard, shaped, transparent framework, alternating in function between mirror and landscape, in fact suggests quite powerfully the model of painting.

And indeed Marcel has just seen in Carpaccio's *Patriarche di Grado* (whose source as a repository of imagery used by Fortuny in creating a dress worn by Albertine I discuss in chapters 6 & 7) a roofscape evoking the kind of tulip garden that Whistler's paintings of Venice resemble. Thus Whistler lies embedded in Carpaccio as Turner lay embedded within Titian:

I looked at the marvellous rose-pink and violet sky and the tall encrusted chimneys silhouetted against it, their flared stacks, blossoming like red tulips, reminiscent of so many Whistlers of Venice.　　(K III 661, P III 646–7).

But the Venetian townscape rapidly becomes a Dutch one:

With their tall, splayed chimneys to which the sun imparts the most vivid pinks, the brightest reds – like a garden flowering above the houses, and flowering in such a variety of tints as to suggest the garden of a tulip-fancier of Delft or Haarlem planted above the town.

(K II 594, P III 650 & P II 572).

The mention of the towns associated with Vermeer and Hals is enough, without mentioning their names, to restructure the metaphor in terms of Dutch painting[15]:

And then the extreme proximity of the houses, with their windows looking across at one another over a common courtyard, makes of each casement the frame in which a cook sits dreamily gazing down at the ground below, or, further off, a girl is having her hair combed by an old woman with a witchlike face, barely distinguishable in the shadow: thus each courtyard provides the neighbours in the adjoining house, [suppressing sound by its width and framing silent gestures in a series of rectangles placed under glass by the closing of the windows,] with an exhibition of a hundred Dutch paintings hung in rows.　　(K II 594, P III 650 & [P II 572]).

The painting reflected an artificial nature evoked by another painting of the landscape, which was as embedded ('incrusté') as one could wish. Now the reference to Dutch painting reasserts the function of embedding itself. Rather than Carpaccio embedding Whistler (as Titian embedded Turner), we have the artist himself, Marcel, creating a framework ('the extreme proximity of the houses [...] makes of each casement, the frame'), but then finding himself mirrored within that frame, the object of the gaze of the girls who step outside their represented role ('the frame in which a cook sits dreamily gazing down'). The girls echo Marcel in their opaque, creative dreaming. We think of the episode of the eagle-ring given to Albertine, where Marcel tries desperately to decipher the image of the eagle and the text of the donor but is left with the vision of a puzzled face, a mirror-image of his own scrutinising (see my chapter 6). Although it is the resemblance of Venetian chimneys to Dutch tulips that introduces Dutch painting here, as early as *Un amour de Swann*, the melody from Vinteuil's sonata, adopted by Swann and Odette as their 'national anthem', was described as framed and embedded within the surrounding texture of the music, in terms of Pieter de Hooch's painting:

He would begin with the sustained tremolos of the violin part which for several bars were heard alone, filling the whole foreground; until suddenly they seemed to draw aside, and – as in those interiors by Pieter de Hooch which are deepened by the narrow frame of a half-opened door, in the far distance, of a different colour, velvety with the radiance of some intervening light – the little phrase appeared, dancing, pastoral, interpolated, episodic, belonging to another world. (K I 238, P I 218).

As with the gaze emanating from the supposedly observed girls, so inside Swann's frame within a frame, violins or doorway, something observed appears to overrun the structure surrounding it, and escape the observer, who fails to dominate or penetrate its microcosmic structure.

Indeed, agonised by the reflection, as it floated by, so near and yet so infinitely remote, that while it was addressed to them it did not know them, he almost regretted that it had a meaning of its own, an intrinsic and unalterable beauty, extraneous to themselves, just as in the jewels given to us, or even in the letters written to us by a woman we love, we find fault with the "water" of the stone, or with the words of the message, because they are not fashioned exclusively from the essence of a transient liaison and a particular person. (K I 238–9, P I 219).

We can see, as Swann cannot, that his regret is an expression of lack of artistic control and creativity as a musical motif refuses to dissolve into passion and obstinately retains its own inassimilable structuring force. Marcel's own Dutch interiors in *La fugitive* are more powerfully reflective: Swann figures one de Hooch painting whose embedded frame yet fails to integrate his love, but Marcel sees 'an exhibition of a hundred Dutch paintings hung in rows'[16] – and 'hung in rows' (*juxtaposés*), both in the real street and the figurative art gallery, must I think imply 'facing' as well as 'side by side', giving us the vertiginous outer spiral of the *mise en abîme* as a veritable hall of mirrors is constituted, each act of perception or representation or creation being in its turn reflected within the frame of another, and so on 'unfolding as though for ever and ever', as Marcel says of his Venetian palaces in his Giotto dream. Proust mentally superimposes the plunging and reechoing depths of a de Hooch interior – say 'The Courtyard of a House in Delft' – on a composite Vermeer image of multiple reflections – say the dreamy 'Lady reading at an open Window', with its oblique, opaque mirroring, and the 'Little Street in Delft', where a row of doorways frames a series of female figures.

Moreover, Marcel's medium is not the music of another creator, but his own subjective, plastic fantasy: girls and glassware, art exhibitions and the Grand Canal, come together to form the substance of the vision, and the structuring force of the vision could be seen to be that of the artisan working on his own material – the 'distension' suddenly billowing out in the hard glass could make us think of Marcel as a glass-blower, seeing his own reflection as he blows his material into shape and creates a hollow form reflecting his activities; and the other great Venetian glasswork, the mosaic, which I posit as a major structuring figure in the *Recherche* (see chapter 8), is temptingly glimpsed in the fragmented, crystalline structure of the whole vision, with Marcel's own perception constantly caught in its midst, like a character from the *Arabian Nights*:

I had plunged into a network of little alleys, or *calli*, packed tightly together and dissecting in all directions with their furrows a chunk of Venice carved out between a canal and the lagoon, as if it had crystallised in accordance with these innumerable, tenuous and minute patterns. Suddenly at the end of one of these alleys, it seemed as though a distension had occurred in the crystallised matter. [...] It was one of those architectural ensembles towards which, in any other town, the streets converge, lead you and point the way. Here it seemed to be deliberately concealed in a labyrinth of alleys, like those palaces in oriental tales whither mysterious agents convey by night a person who, brought back home before daybreak, can never find his way back to the magic dwelling which he ends by believing that he visited only in a dream. (K III 665, P III 650–1).

Marcel is lost in his own creation, rather than excluded from somebody else's, as Swann was. The whole structure of the reversal of

perspective as the viewer becomes framed within his own vision
and the narrator makes a frame around his own story, is, as we
may have just noticed, likened to a famous Oriental narrative.

The Oriental masterpiece is evoked perhaps partly because of the
Oriental associations of Venice (exploited in Carpaccio's paintings,
cf. my chapter 7), but it has also been announced in *La Prisonnière*
as a motif of creativity and reflexive consciousness.[17] Listening to
Vinteuil's 'septet' without knowing its identity, Marcel suddenly
hears the musical phrase from Vinteuil's earlier work, the 'sonata':

> The concert began; I did not know what was being played; I found myself
> in a strange land. Where was I to place it? Who was the composer? I longed
> to know, and, seeing nobody near me whom I could ask, I should have
> liked to be a character in those *Arabian Nights* which I never tired of reading
> and in which, in moments of uncertainty, there appears a genie, or a maiden
> of ravishing beauty, invisible to everyone else but not to the perplexed
> hero to whom she reveals exactly what he wishes to learn.
>
> (K III 250, P III 248–9).

What masquerades as a chance association for Marcel (wishing for
a genie because he has been reading the *Arabian Nights*) becomes
for the reader an invitation to see that the experience of responding
to art presents Marcel with the problem of his own creativity, as
well as a key to its resolution through an understanding of how
he is held captive within the structure of other works of art. The
'genie' who might help explain the mystery does in fact come in
La Prisonnière, in the guise of recognition of a repeated motif:

> And indeed at that very moment I was favoured with just such a magical
> apparition. As when, in a stretch of country which one thinks one does
> not know and which in fact one has approached from a new direction,
> after turning a corner one finds oneself suddenly emerging on to a road
> every inch of which is familiar, but one had simply not been in the habit
> of approaching it that way, one suddenly says to oneself: "Why, this is
> the lane that leads to the garden gate of my friends the X—s; I'm only
> two minutes from their house," and there, indeed, is their daughter who
> has come out to greet one as one goes by; so, all of a sudden, I found
> myself, in the midst of this music that was new to me, right in the heart
> of Vinteuil's sonata; and, more marvellous than any adolescent girl, the
> little phrase.
>
> (K III 250–1, P III 249).

Teasingly Proust suggests within a metaphor the final rejoining of 'le côté de Guermantes' and 'le côté de Méséglise', and the supremacy of art over desire ('more marvellous than any adolescent girl'). Later, in the text from *La fugitive* in question, the landscape is still permeated with hundreds of girls, who merge with the structure instead of yielding to it, and seem to lead Marcel away from art:

'But, far more than certain places, it was the desire not to lose forever certain women that kept me while in Venice in a state of agitation which became febrile' [...].   (K III 666, P III 651).

The genie comes when called, but now seems to mislead:

The next day, I set out in quest of my beautiful nocturnal *piazza*, following *calle* after *calle* which were exactly like one another and refused to give me the smallest piece of information, except such as would lead me further astray. Sometimes a vague landmark which I seemed to recognise led me to suppose that I was about to see appear, in its seclusion, solitude and silence, the beautiful exiled *piazza*. At that moment, some evil genie which had assumed the form of a new *calle* made me unwittingly retrace my steps, and I found myself suddenly brought back to the Grand Canal.

(K III 665–6, P III 651).

With a delightful inverse mirror-image, the secret square sought by the lost hero and his good genie, has become transposed into a princess sequestered by a bad genie. The retreat from the good genie who guided Marcel through the Vinteuil septet is only apparent, however. Here the stakes are much higher, since Marcel is exploring his own creativity rather than his response to someone else's, and, in his dreams, fantasies, wanderings and desires, Marcel is moving ever closer to the crises and discoveries of *Le temps retrouvé*, and the very resistance of his mind to its own structurings and imaginings shows that he is nearer to the heart of his own subjective creativity. There are at other moments in Venice hints that the good narrative genie from the *Arabian Nights* is looking after him, even when he is not seeking art or lost time but simply 'Venetian women':

There were many things that I made no attempt to identify in the excitement I felt as I went in search of Venetian women.

My gondola followed the course of the small canals; like the mysterious hand of a genie leading me through the maze of this oriental city, they seemed, as I advanced, to be cutting a path for me through the heart of a crowded quarter which they bisected, barely parting, with a slender furrow arbitrarily traced, the tall houses with their tiny Moorish windows and as though the magic guide had been holding a candle in his hand and were lighting the way for me, they kept casting ahead of them a ray of sunlight for which they cleared a route.   (K III 641, P III 626–7).

The *Arabian Nights* are the archetypal story within a story. Sheherezade is both anguished heroine and necessarily compulsive narrator. Each night she must suspend her own destiny and insert within it the incomplete but hypnotic form of another. The chain of her 'récits' (the 'and one' after the 'Thousand' of the French title, *Les mille et une nuits*, suggesting infinity) then suggests that her own destiny is an endless reflection of these embedded narratives. Thus Marcel dreaming of Combray and careering after Venetian shopgirls both suspends and creates narrative. Through the long, repetitive nights of his relationship with Albertine and the intense evenings of Venetian tourism, in the overt exploration of memory in bed when he recalls Combray as in the masked explorations of consciousness which occur in passages such as the Venetian dream (K II 147–8, P II 145–6) and the Venetian fantasia (K III 665–6, P III 650–1) which I have been analysing, Marcel explores his own story, putting off the final moment when the whole story will have to have an answer, until he finally realises that he has written it in the very exploration of the 'slender furrow' of narrative whilst waiting for that answer.

The critic hopes that Proust's own conclusion to the *Arabian Nights* theme will eventually reveal what he himself has 'arbitrarily traced':

But my task was longer than his, my words had to reach more than a single person. My task was long. By day, the most I could hope for was to try to sleep. If I worked, it would be only at night. But I should need many nights, a hundred perhaps, or even a thousand. And I should live in the anxiety of not knowing whether the master of my destiny might not prove less indulgent than the Sultan Shahriyar, whether in the morning, when I broke off my story, he would consent to a further reprieve and permit me to resume my narrative the following evening. Not that I had the slightest pretension to be writing a new version, in any way, of the

Thousand and One Nights, or of that other book written by night, Saint-Simon's *Memoirs*, or of any of those books which I had loved.

(K III 1101–2, P III 1043).

Each of Sheherezade's stories, each of Marcel's passages, must mirror the final goal in miniature, but not quite perfectly – to conclude prematurely would be to preclude conclusion. And thus the critic's discourse embedding Proust's structure must be allowed to carry some overarching flaw, through which the mirrored structure of Proust's text will flaunt its uncontainable completeness. For – 'as Elstir had found with Chardin – you can make a new version of what you love only by first renouncing it' (K III 1102, P III 1043).

6

Fortuny (I): a phoenix too frequent

On ne peut refaire ce qu'on aime qu'en le renonçant.

Marcel Proust

Mariano Fortuny y Madrazo, son of a Spanish painter, was married to the sister of Proust's friend Reynaldo Hahn. Recent exhibitions in the Museo Fortuny in Venice show the range of interests of this energetic innovator.[1] He was an early experimenter with colour dia-positives, produced naturalistic photographic portraits and land-scapes in an age dominated by pomp and twee. He photographed a princess for a butter advert in 1899, and photographed a series of strikingly relaxed nudes in 1920. He revolutionised theatrical settings at La Fenice and other theatres, with a mixture of illusionistic tricks, of ultra-realistic all-enveloping settings, and an avant-garde functional symbolism. He produced his friend Hofmannsthal's plays, and a complete representation of Wagner's *Ring*. He invented a rather grandiose system of indirect lighting for stage and photogra-phy, the light being diffused by passing through a giant fabric cupola. But it is for his stage costumes and town gowns that Proust elects Fortuny to a starring role in his novel. In 1910 Fortuny patented a printing and dyeing process in Paris. He dressed Eleonora Duse, Sarah Bernhardt, Réjane, and Isadora Duncan, he decorated the gaming room of the Hotel Excelsior on the Lido in Venice. At the height of his fame, in 1919, he opened a dress shop in the Boule-vard Haussmann. By one of the ironies life reserves the right to afford art, he designed the lighting for some paintings in Venice mentioned in *La Recherche*, after Proust's death.[2]

Proust's first sign of interest in Fortuny appears in his series of letters to Maria de Madrazo (née Hahn) in 1916.[3] In another inscrut-able figure of fate Proust, who had lived at no. 102 Boulevard

Haussmann from 1907 until the end of May 1919, then had to move out in the very year that Fortuny opened his shop in the same street. He then spent the next four months, from 1 June to 1 October, in an apartment at 8 bis rue Laurent Hamelin, a building owned and inhabited by the actress Réjane herself.[4] Indeed, he was able to stay until the end of September mainly because Réjane was away visiting Venice in September[5]... But beyond these amusing coincidences, Proust's main interest in Fortuny was as a reviver of antique motifs.

In the first instance it was perceptive of Proust to see that this modernistic *touche-à-tout* was a profound reviver of tradition. Fortuny performed a veritable resurrection of authentic Greek costumes, designed after the originals, for Isadora Duncan. He deliberately raided medieval Oriental tapestry designs and Venetian Renaissance painting for motifs for his materials and stage costumes and fashionable dresses.

In Proust's work the Fortuny dress is a sign of ostentatious wealth, like a yacht (K III 154, P III 157), as well as a sign of erotic generosity, display and possession: Marcel asks Albertine to parade before him in the dresses or even merely draped in the material, as a model for his erotic delectation and aesthetic contemplation (K III 377–8, P III 370).

Most significantly, the Fortuny dress provides a link between eroticism and art. It clothes the desirable Albertine with motifs recalling Venice, the Venice of Carpaccio and Veronese, according to Elstir, who announces the imminent arrival of the dresses in Paris:

I hear that a Venetian artist, called Fortuny, has rediscovered the secret of the craft, and that in a few years' time women will be able to parade around, and better still to sit at home, in brocades as sumptuous as those that Venice adorned for her patrician daughters with patterns brought from the Orient. (K I 960, P I 899).

Elstir describes the women portrayed in Carpaccio's paintings as wearing cherry brocade, green damask, black sleeves slashed with white, and bordered with pearls or decorated with 'guipures' (open lace with no backing):

The ships ... displayed ladies in cerise brocade and green damask close under the balconies incrusted with multi-coloured marble from which other ladies leaned to gaze at them, in gowns with black sleeves slashed with white, stitched with pearls or bordered with lace.   (K I 959, P I 898–9).

Although it is the ambassadorial sequences of Carpaccio's *Legend of St Ursula* cycle which Elstir refers to, it is Carpaccio's painting in the Correr museum, *Le Cortigiane*, which springs to mind. This painting is mentioned later by Marcel to Albertine because of the courtisans' resemblance to Dostoevsky's mysterious heroines (K III, 384, P III 377).[6] The ladies have black, lacey sleeves, slashed open over a white lining, and bordered with pearls, whilst their skirts are one red, the other cream with a green border. But the evocation of artistic structuring is not merely a question of referring to Venetian costume and art, however. The ships 'display' women as the women 'display' dresses (Proust's 'portaient' means both 'bore' and 'wore'). Balconies appear 'incrusted' equally with multicoloured marble and women. The women are framed within decorative, coloured dresses. A whole principle of *mise en abîme* is suggested in Proust's style.

Elstir's forecast of a revival by Fortuny of Venetian costumes and motifs is fulfilled later when Oriane de Guermantes appears in an evening gown 'of a magnificent Tiepolo red' (K II 686, P II 661), and this red is recalled by the 'Tiepolo pink',[7] or cherry pink lining of the sleeves of a blue and gold dress worn by Albertine (K III 401, P III 394). The dresses tend to be described in terms of a simple colour, a vague style – they are from 'old Venetian models' (K III 26, P III 33), a gold-streaked dressing gown is of imprecise colour: 'dark, fluffy, speckled, streaked with gold like a butterfly's wing' (K III 36, P III 43), another gown is 'blue and gold' (K III 401, 406, P III 394, 399), and the decoration is oriental on a gown 'covered with Arab ornamentation ... like the bindings in the Ambrosian library' (K III 401, P III 394). There is pearl and gold embroidery on the collar or the sleeve (K III 662, P III 647). Ultimately, the robes may simply be blue (K III 412, P III 405), the blue of the sea or the sky.[8]

For the major function of the dresses is to revive Venice. Although as we have seen Marcel drapes Albertine in this finery partly to enjoy her erotic parade (K III 377–8, P III 370), there is also in the drapery a stimulus to Marcel's erotic longings and aesthetic

4   Mariano Fortuny, Gown, Museo Fortuny, Venice. (Photo P. Collier).

ambitions which take him beyond the present body and person of Albertine. A blue and gold dress evokes the Grand Canal through the colour of sunlight on water (K III 406, P III 399), and the oriental motifs are surely deliberately literary, attractively and exotically literary, in their resemblance to the designs on the bindings of precious Oriental books:

The Fortuny gown which Albertine was wearing that evening seemed to me the tempting phantom of that invisible Venice. It was covered with Arab ornamentation, like the Venetian palaces hidden like sultan's wives behind a screen of pierced stone, like the bindings in the Ambrosian Library.

(K III 401, P III 394).

The Fortuny dress evokes Venice, in the mode of erotic temptation. The sexual desire which the dress should focus on Albertine's forms is transported instead onto the more interesting volumes of Italian libraries,[9] onto Venetian structures seen as excitingly forbidden, veiled harem women. They become the dresses of the Doges' ladies (K III 376, P III 369), their blue and gold evokes spring in Venice (K III 419, P III 412), their very display of Venetian finery instead

82

of rendering Albertine more lovable exacerbates Marcel's realisation of the excitement of Venice that he is renouncing in order to stay with her:

To be on the safe side, I heaped more and more presents on her. As regards the Fortuny gowns, we had at length decided upon one in blue and gold lined with pink which was just ready [...] It was the very evening on which Albertine had put on for the first time the indoor gown in gold and blue by Fortuny which, by reminding me of Venice, made me feel all the more strongly what I was sacrificing for her, who showed no corresponding gratitude towards me. (K III 401, P III 394).

As long as they are being worn by Albertine, the robes remind Marcel of Venice obliquely, through their source in Venetian paintings or motifs.[10] Conversely, once Albertine has disappeared, the very blue of the sky – 'the blueness of an insect's wing' – will remind him of her (K III 491, P III 481), and in Venice itself the coat worn by a Compagnone della Calza in Carpaccio's *Patriarche di Grado* will bring nostalgia and pain through its revival of the memory of a dress that Albertine wore (K III 662, P III 647).[11]

The main thematic power of these painterly costumes and motifs designed by Fortuny does in fact derive from the fact that they are already themselves resurrected, twice resurrected, in the first place. Initially, beautiful designs and colours, despite the ephemerality of their fashion, have survived through art – Titian or Veronese or Carpaccio confer a certain immortality on the fleeting flesh and fabric they celebrate – and then, centuries later, the dormant artistic pattern can be resuscitated anew by the artistry of a Fortuny: 'the magnificent garments of the women of Carpaccio's and Titian's day ... rising from their ashes' (K III 375, P III 368). This resurrection is given major thematic prominence by its association with the phoenix and with St Mark's Basilica in Venice. The death and rebirth of the Phoenix is evoked in the phrase 'rising from their ashes', but this motif is given wider significance:

for everything must return in time, as it is written beneath the vaults of St Mark's, and proclaimed, as they drink from the urns of marble and jasper of the Byzantine capitals, by the birds which symbolise at once death and resurrection. (K III 375–7, P III 368).

5   Vittore Carpaccio. *The patriarch of Grado*, Accademia, Venice.

The reference to the phoenix as a metaphor for the resuscitation of the motifs, leads the narrative by a process of metonymy to the birds portrayed in mosaic or sculpture at St Mark's. I myself have found no discernible phoenixes at St Mark's, but there are many peacocks busily drinking in urns of marble, jasper and mosaic, on the floor as well as on the walls and, possibly, on the capitals. Peacocks, too, are a symbol of resurrection.

The phoenix is a well-known Christian and Venetian symbol, but it is not actually very prevalent in the city. The 'Fenice' theatre, burnt down in 1836 but rebuilt in facsimile,[12] is the central, generative image; there is one on the walls of the 'Dogana'; and there is a phoenix symbolising the Christian resurrection carved on a tombstone now displayed in the Correr museum. But it is everywhere the peacock, its rival symbol of immortality and resurrection, which triumphs in Venice. On either side of the chancel screen in Torcello cathedral a pair of bas-relief peacocks supping from a chalice guards the approach to the altar,[13] and St Mark's (despite being a veritable menagerie of gryphons, John's eagles, Mark's lions and doves of the Holy Spirit) reserves pride of place to two enormous pairs of mosaic peacocks, a pair on either side of the floor of the nave, as well as displaying one bas-relief pair on the parapet of the first-floor gallery and another couple of pairs inset in the outer north-west wall. Outside the north front of the Basilica is a peacock surmounting a globe, symbolising the triumph of the spirit over the world of earthly desires, and there is another pair of these carved beside the altar steps.

Ruskin in his *Stones of Venice* copies the twin pair inset in the outer wall over the north-west door.[14] There is a brace of drinking peacocks above a pair of similar but intertwined birds, and he copies in the same illustration carvings of another pair of peacocks drinking from a chalice they perch on, and also a pair of birds linked at the waist which are either a double eagle or twin phoenixes (it is difficult to tell whether they are on fire or merely have spiky feathers).[15] The importance of the bird imagery is underlined by Ruskin in his main description of St Mark's:

Under foot and over head, a continual succession of crowded imagery, one picture passing into another, as in a dream; forms beautiful and terrible mixed together; dragons and serpents, and ravening beasts of prey, and graceful birds that in the midst of them drink from running fountains and feed from vases of crystal; the passions and the pleasures of human life symbolised together, and the mystery of its redemption.

(Morris 84, Whittick 203, *Stones of Venice*, Tr. Ed. p. 109).

Proust prepares us to find symbolic significance in the peacock by its association with the church in *Du Côté de chez Swann*. He comments on a stained-glass window 'où dominait le bleu', but which becomes transformed either by the sunlight or his gaze into a peacock's tail:

Byzantine Sculpture.

6   John Ruskin. Byzantine sculpture (from *The Stones of Venice*).

the next instant it had taken on the shimmering brilliance of a peacock's tail, then quivered and rippled in a flaming and fantastic shower that streamed from the groin of the dark and stony vault.   (K I 65, P I 60).

The peacock's tail has become a waterfall and then stalactites. And then again the blue and gold waters and shadows of Venice seem to be prefigured:

a fleeting smile from the sun, which could be seen and felt as well here, in the soft, blue stream with which it bathed the jewelled windows, as on the pavement of the Square or the straw of the market-place; and [...] it would console me for the blackness and bareness of the earth outside by quickening into blossom, as in some springtime in old history among the heirs of Saint Louis, this dazzling, gilded carpet of forget-me-nots in glass.[16]   (K I 65, P I 60).

And long after the visit to Venice, in *Le Temps retrouvé* when the Venetian episode is recalled via the Guermantes' paving-stone, a table-napkin evokes a peacock's-tail ocean, which is actually a reminiscence of the seaside at Balbec, but which continues the exploration of Marcel's Venice-based resurrection of his past:

the napkin which I had used to wipe my mouth had precisely the same degree of stiffness and starchedness as the towel with which I had found it so awkward to dry my face as I stood in front of the window on the first day of my arrival at Balbec, and this napkin now, in the library of the Prince de Guermantes's house, unfolded for me – concealed within its smooth surfaces and its folds – the plumage of an ocean green and blue like the tail of a peacock.   (K III 901, P III 869).

I have already mentioned briefly in chapters 2 & 3 the eagle imagery surrounding Albertine. And before she is associated with the phoenix or peacock imagery, she is associated with the image of a spread eagle on a ring (K III 57, P III 63). A second ring acquired by Albertine has a motif not at first decoded by Marcel, who sees only a ruby, surrounded by markings in which he deciphers a man's face – 'I can't quite make out what that is carved round the ruby, it looks like a man's grinning face.' (K III 162–3, P III 165).

After Albertine's disappearance Françoise discovers the same eagle engraved on both rings, and mocks Marcel's determination to see just 'une espèce de tête d'homme qui est ciselée', as she does his protest that the rings were acquired from two different sources, Albertine having bought one and received the other from her aunt:

there's the same eagle on both, the same initials inside. . . ."

"A man's head? Where did Monsieur see that? I had only to put on my specs to see at once that it was one of the eagle's wings. If Monsieur takes his magnifying glass, he'll see the other wing on the other side, and the head and the beak in the middle. You can count every feather. Oh, it's a fine piece of work." (K III 472, P III 463).

Larkin Price points out that the eagle plunging its beak into the ruby symbolises the effect of its discovery, like a dagger in the heart:

Shattered, holding the two rings in my hand, I stared at that pitiless eagle whose beak was rending my heart, whose wings, chiselled in high relief, had borne away the trust that I still retained in my mistress, in whose claws my tortured mind was unable to escape for an instant from the incessantly recurring questions concerning the stranger whose name the eagle doubtless symbolised though without allowing me to decipher it [...] the eagle appeared to be dipping its beak in the bright blood of the ruby.

(Price, p. 256; K III 474, P 464–5).

Perhaps one might complement this insight with the observation that the ring contains a more elaborate and covert level of symbolism. The narrator, Marcel, has obscured the true interpretation of the narrative, by misreading the motif as that of a grimacing face. But this misreading comes close to the truth concealed in this deliberately inscrutable eagle symbol, for the eagle represents the person who gave it to Albertine (probably Léa, although this is never clearly established). Only this person is a woman. So that Marcel has only misread the gender of the symbol, as long as he misreads the equivocal sexual identity of Albertine. But the eagle also chokes this effort to decode, and thus the narrator in his strangulated misreading perfectly mirrors his *own* puzzled face.

Price points out that Françoise's use of a magnifying glass echoes the microscopic examination of the narrative's symbolism. I would add that the text's *mise en abîme* here not only mirrors its own unraveling of enigmatic reality, it alerts us to the likelihood that the eagle's beak plunged in the blood of the ruby may function as a symbol of the pain of writing about the self – the investigating quill stabbing into the heart rather than into ink – as well as a *mise en abîme* wherein that suffering itself secretes a jewel within a jewel (the ruby within the ring), a miniature work of art inset within the greater work, and which helps to decode it.

Within the economy of a text working in terms of resurrection and repetition, it becomes important then that one of the moments of revival of thoughts about Albertine in Venice in *La Fugitive* concerns the eagle motif seen at San Giorgio degli Schiavoni:

Another time, in San Giorgio degli Schiavoni, an eagle accompanying one of the Apostles, and conventionalised in the same manner, revived the memory and almost the suffering caused by the two rings the similarity of which Françoise had revealed to me, and as to which I had never learned who had given them to Albertine.   (K III 656, P III 641).

The eagle is now associated with the sequence of Carpaccio paintings at San Giorgio, and Carpaccio is the painter whose artistic motifs Fortuny has resurrected. Moreover, the eagle in the context is the eagle of St John the Evangelist, which again emphasises a Christian resurrectional dimension. In fact this rebirth of the memory of Albertine is I think a deliberate purification of the eagle as ambiguity/jealousy motif. It happens just before the crucial passage where Marcel enters the Baptistery with his mother and a volume of Ruskin and readjusts his ideas and feelings about art, desire and memory. The 'eagle' passage continues immediately as if it has been an abortive renaissance of Albertine, to be followed by a more nearly successful revival of his love for her as Albertine herself appears to rise phoenix-like from the dead in the telegram Marcel reads:

"My dear friend, you think me dead, forgive me, I am quite alive, I long to see you, talk about marriage, when do you return? Affectionately. Albertine."   (K III 656, P III 641).

Even here however, and even before he finds out that Albertine is genuinely dead, and the signature was really Gilberte's, Marcel finds that there is no resuscitation of his amorous thoughts and sensory reactions:

Albertine had been no more to me than a bundle of thoughts, and she had survived her physical death so long as those thoughts were alive in me; on the other hand, now that those thoughts were dead, Albertine did not rise again for me with the resurrection of her body.

(K III 656, P III 641–2).

This is a moment of great psychological importance for Marcel, who realises that he cannot resurrect his past: that we all become different people with the passage of time, and are disturbed not to recognise our altered faces in the mirror:

This is shattering because its message is: "the man that I was, the fair-haired young man, no longer exists, I am another person." [...] And the reason why one is not distressed is the same, namely that the self which has been eclipsed—momentarily in this latter case and when it is a question of character, permanently in the former case and when the passions are involved—is not there to deplore the other. [...] I should have been incapable of resuscitating Albertine because I was incapable of resuscitating myself, of resuscitating the self of those days. (K III 657, P III 642).

And yet only a few pages later there will be the feeling of eternal salvation and fixity that will lay the ground for the resuscitation of the past self which occurs in *Le Temps retrouvé*, and give the lie to the 'general law of oblivion' into which his love for Albertine appears doomed to slide (K III 659, P III 644). The passage that deals with Marcel's Ruskinian pilgrimage to the Baptistery with his mother (K III 660–2, P III 645–7) will be the subject of my chapter 8.

L. Price and D. de Agostini rather uncritically accept that the bird imagery of the Fortuny dresses is phoenix imagery.[17] Of course Proust may have mistaken the eagles, doves and peacocks on the premises of St Mark's for phoenixes. I think it more likely that he uses the phoenix imagery deliberately at the outset, and then knowingly uses an ambiguous formula which preserves the more familiar symbolism of the phoenix but integrates the symbolism into the more systematic use of the eagle and peacock imagery elsewhere in the novel. We must not forget that Proust may be *creating* as much as copying Fortuny dresses, just as he creates Impressionist paintings for Elstir, and there is a danger that critics who reconstruct these paintings piece by piece from Proust's myriad sources may misrepresent his creativity.

For the power of the symbolism of the Fortuny dress lies in its intricate conjugation of death and desire, art and resurrection. On a dress worn by Albertine as Marcel tries to embrace her the birds are referred to as 'oiseaux fatidiques':

"Since you're being kind enough to stay here a moment to console me, you ought to take off your gown, it's too hot, too stiff, I dare not approach you for fear of crumpling that fine stuff, and there are those fateful birds between us. Undress, my darling."   (K III 406, P III 400).

It is not just that the phoenix/peacock image implies the presence of death as a condition for any regeneration. The attractive, peacock-like erotic display of the dress is mortal because of its very artistic fragility, the birds appear to threaten hell-fire as a concomitant of erotic coupling, the dress's very stiffness is a perfectly ambiguous conjunction of the erection and the rigor mortis which the naked prostrate body would intimate in this perspective. And of course one could see the fear of crushing the birds as an elaborate projection of unconscious fears of sexuality in Marcel, rather unconvincingly overlaid by his conscious enactment of the role of the heavy-breathing seducer.

The ambiguity of the phoenix/peacock imagery and even its mimetic or fantastical status, is also important when Marcel embraces her without trying to remove the garment:

I kissed her then a second time, pressing to my heart the shimmering golden azure of the Grand Canal and the mating birds, symbols of death and resurrection. But for the second time, instead of returning my kiss, she drew away with the sort of instinctive and baleful obstinacy of animals that feel the hand of death.   (K III 406, P III 399).

Again the symbolism suggests death as a necessary implication of the erotic union. Both the phoenix and the peacock of course in Christian iconography evidently imply not mainly a physical rebirth (except in so far as Christ himself was reincarnated) but above all the death of the bodily and the rebirth of the spiritual. In this passage the shimmering blue and gold colours and the erotic pairing of the birds is typical of the peacock and the dove, whereas the reaction of Albertine, compared to that of a frightened animal (or bird), and thus breaking up the figure of the pair of love-birds, evokes an image of the creature being destroyed, an image more redolent of the fire-ringed phoenix. It is as if Albertine understands the profound dangers of Marcel's desire (which have little to do with the superficial difficulties of seduction). The real drive of Marcel will eventually be revealed as the transcendence of the bodily and erotic in favour of a regeneration on the plane of the spiritual and artistic.[18] It is as if Albertine feels instinctively that Marcel's possession of her will lead to his dissatisfaction with her (since he seeks essential knowledge as well as total physical possession, which he wrongly sees as a means of acquiring the former). It is clear enough that even in his most urgent erotic thrust Marcel is grasping at Venice ('pressing up against my body the shimmering golden azure of the Grand Canal') and resurrection, rather than at the person of Albertine. The coupling of the birds on the dress is a felicitous image perhaps suggested to Proust by the fact that the peacocks of St Mark's are nearly always in pairs, as are the doves, which are primarily signs of the Holy Spirit in the Church, but who are just as commonly symbols of love in general. It would be more in the spirit of Proust's creativity, however, to suppose that the phoenix/peacock motifs are separate on the material, and that we are invited to imagine the embrace itself crushing together in the folds of the cloth birds which are separately drawn.[19] The embrace causes the coupling, but it is a coupling which stifles. And on a symbolic level, this reminds us that the basely erotic is commonly seen in religious terms to be death to the spirit, and in terms of *La Recherche*, Swann's infatuation with Odette and Marcel's with Albertine are seen to impede their progress with Vermeer and with Venice respectively. We have already noted how the symbolism of eagle, phoenix and peacock is intricately interrelated, rather than compartmentalised. In this context it is interesting to remember that the medallion recorded by Ruskin from outside the north-west door of St Mark's showing two pairs of peacocks, shows the upper pair as facing each other, drinking from the chalice, whereas the lower pair, perhaps peahens, are interlaced in a way that could be described as 'accouplés' ('mating'). (The standard, facing peacocks would not be easily describable as 'accouplés'). The interlaced birds form a common Venetian motif, alongside the more dignified motif of the facing birds. As the second eagle-ring compounded the ambiguity and treachery of Albertine, so the imagery of ambiguously intertwined female birds could well be another subliminal evocation of Albertine's equivocal sexuality.[20]

Behind the pessimistic symbolism, which seems to suggest a spiritual salvation at heavy personal cost, there is however a whole dimension of aesthetic transcendence suggested. This capacity of art to survive, to revive, and to transcend will be the subject of the next chapter.

7

Fortuny (II): Carpaccio's material

Tout comme l'avenir, ce n'est pas tout à la fois, mais
grain par grain qu'on goûte le passé.   Marcel Proust

Apart from one or two glancing references to Titian and Veronese,
it is Carpaccio who in Proust's text operates the structural transformation of decoration into art, of desire into resurrection, of theme
into *mise en abîme*. He is introduced in *Du Côté de chez Swann* as
a painter, like Titian, who should be appreciated in Venice rather
than in the Louvre, and the Carpaccio paintings in the Scuola San
Giorgio dei (sic) Schiavoni are mentioned in the same breath as
the 'Titian of the Frari' (the *Assumption of the Virgin* in Santa Maria
Gloriosa dei Frari), as the archetypal Venetian masterpiece (K 1475,
P 1440–1). But where (as we have seen) the Titian references remain
obstinately undercut by authorial irony, the Carpaccio allusions take
on a richness and complexity equalled by no other real painter mentioned in the *Recherche*. (The fictitious Elstir is another matter.) A
specific reference in *Contre Sainte-Beuve*[1] to the *Dream of St Ursula*
(part of the *Sant' Orsola* sequence in the Accademia) becomes in
the *Recherche* a more general reference to Oriane de Guermantes
by the young Marcel, using the most lyrical terms, as inspired by
Wagner's music and Carpaccio's painting:

the sun [...] shed a geranium glow over the red carpet laid down for the
wedding, across which Mme de Guermantes was smilingly advancing, and
covered its woollen texture with a nap of rosy velvet, a bloom of luminosity,
that sort of tenderness, of solemn sweetness in the pomp of a joyful celebration, which characterise certain pages of *Lohengrin*, certain paintings
by Carpaccio, and make us understand how Baudelaire was able to apply
to the sound of the trumpet the epithet "delicious."   (K 1194, P 1178).

Proust's admiration is clear from his including Carpaccio in this
Holy Trio of artists whose other two members are Wagner and

Baudelaire. It is typical of Proust's brilliant regressional structuring that the superposed layers of diaphanous pink light, and of festive formality, which overlay the vision of Oriane in church and the works of Wagner and Carpaccio, are subtly rooted in the structure of Carpaccio's own narrative painting: Oriane's radiant progress over a red carpet reenacts the whole sumptuous procession of St Ursula; the trumpets attributed to Baudelaire are literally present in Carpaccio; at the same time Baudelaire's synaesthetic metaphor alerts us to the whole synaesthetic structure of Proust's conceit, with its interweaving of colour and emotion, its implicit description of painting and music in terms of each other.

The painting from the *Sant' Orsola* cycle which comes immediately to mind is the *Incontro dei Fidanzati*, with its sumptuous procession along a gangway draped with Persian carpets towards a stairway which flowers into a spiralling fanfare of trumpets, with its juxtaposed and superimposed planes.

Later, in *A l'ombre des jeunes filles en fleurs*, Elstir's full-scale analysis of Carpaccio's art evokes various paintings from the sequence, where the ships framed by the painting appear to frame within themselves a miniature Venetian townscape in their turn: 'The ships were massive, built like pieces of architecture, and seemed almost amphibious, like lesser Venices set in the heart of the greater' (K I 959, P I 898) – true enough of the *Incontro dei Fidanzati*, where the central galleon, tilted for loading, is the same size as the nearby castle and mountain, and where a galleon on the left appears so set in the land that it sprouts towers. And in the *Arrivo dei Pellegrini a Colonia*, a staggered succession of stately galleons recedes from the structure of the vessel in the foreground (which is larger than the buildings of Cologne), through a gradually diminishing series of mirror images, which miniature galleons miraculously prolong and echo the apparently boatlike floating structure of the fortified bridge of the town, which then is brought symphonically towards the foreground in a series of magnifications of the same structure in the shape of castle battlements. The *Incontro dei Fidanzati* seems almost literally described, with its boats structured and inhabited like small cities:

moored to the banks by hanging stages decked with crimson satin and

7 Vittore Carpaccio. *The meeting of the betrothed couple,* Accademia, Venice.

8   Vittore Carpaccio. *The arrival of the pilgrims at Cologne*, Accademia, Venice.

Persian carpets, they displayed ladies in cerise brocade and green damask close under the balconies incrusted with multi-coloured marble from which other ladies leaned to gaze at them, in gowns with black sleeves slashed with white, stitched with pearls or bordered with lace. You couldn't tell where the land finished and the water began, what was still the palace or already the ship, the caravel, the galley, the Bucintoro.   (K 1959, P 1898).

Two or three series of 'ponts volants' in the *Incontro* lead the protagonists at street level over the water, and the transgression of the boundary between sea and land (so central to Elstir's own painting, as exemplified in *Le Port de Carquethuit*)[2] is further perpetrated by the draping of this waterbound highway, traversing the whole front of the picture, with rich drawing-room 'tapis persans', hung sideways for display as on some interior wall.[3] Meanwhile the real quayside in the background floats thinly out towards the much more substantial embarcations, giving the impression that the foundations of the town resemble a dangerously wafer-like raft. From the betrothed couple on the gangplank in a virtuoso flourish of trumpets the crowd and the carpets recede in a spiral, to be finally echoed in miniature in the balconies of the marble-encrusted palace behind. Rarely has painting shown such narrative and structural sophistication. In the two paintings mentioned, as in the others of the cycle, the temporal narrative sequence is transposed into a spatial progression, but each successive displacement of the narrative is in fact a condensed miniature of the structure of the previous scene, and yet at the same time linked to the previous temporal structure by some spatial allusion – thus for instance we can follow the progress of the *pellegrini* in a circle, moving away through the diminishing succession of boats, then returning through the widening layers of buildings, and yet there is a neat landscape and seascape link across the surface of the painting, literally straddled by a youth and his dog, and a dramatic foreshortening of temporal perspective, as the Huns read the letter announcing the departure of St Ursula and her virgins at the same time as these begin their journey. Thus too we see in the *Incontro* a staggered series of castles merging into a diminishing series of galleons echoing their structures and then widening out into buildings, across the the back of the painting, laterally, while a theory of people loops and snakes in uninterrupted procession from both sides of the middle of the picture, via the sea on the left and seafront balconies on the right, and joining in the middle in the amphibious compromise of the tapestry-draped pontoons.

Thus against these contrapuntal temporal and spatial continua we pick out the beautiful visual and narrative patterns, rhythmical variations on a motif, as the same characters, Ereo and Ursula, appear and disappear in varying steps as if picked out in an elaborate dance by stroboscopic lights, a silent movie camera, or a magic lantern . . .

9   Vittore Carpaccio. *The dream of St Ursula*, Accademia, Venice.

Small wonder that Proust, whose own narrative beneath the rich
varnish of its unhurried syntax keeps readjusting in different postures
varying versions of the same figures at different times and in different
situations, should have picked on the image of the *mise en abîme*
as practised by Carpaccio as the emblem of the art of his exemplary
artist Elstir, and as a miniature emblem of his own text, with its
beautifully controlled intimations of infinity inscribed within the
circle of the dreamer's world. The self-reflecting dreamer is exemplified in the transcendental calm of the dream of St Ursula, who calls
forth in her dream the image of an angel (apparently conjured up

10   Vittore Carpaccio. *The departure of the English ambassadors*, Accademia,
Venice.

in Ursula's dream from the book left open on her table) ready to
dictate through her quill the text of the dream that narrates her,
and thus stepping outside the framework of the dream in an inverse
mise en abîme which echoes Proust's text. Similarly, the scribe at
the still centre of the *Congedo degli ambasciatori inglesi* sits poised
as in eternity in perfect equilibrium between receiving dictation and
creating through his narrative the stylised, frozen actions that sur-
round him.

Elstir's analysis of the metaphorical transformations operated between sea and land in Carpaccio's paintings, and the *mise en abîme* which he identifies in the paintings ('like lesser Venices set in the heart of the greater') and which I have emphasised should guide our reading of the reference to Carpaccio in *Le Côté de Guermantes*. In a further development of the *Contre Sainte-Beuve* draft, what had been an insufferably precious and linear comparison of the narrator's imagination (depicted contemplating the Guermantes lineage) to a plane representation in stained glass of a family tree, now becomes a deliberate evocation of *mise en abîme* (as in the image of a reliquary):

Sometimes it was more than a simple relic that I saw. [...] At once I was lost in contemplation of a reliquary such as Carpaccio or Memling used to paint, from its first panel in which the princess, at the wedding festivities of her brother the Duc d'Orléans, appeared wearing a plain garden dress to indicate her ill-humour at having seen her ambassadors, who had been sent to sue on her behalf for the hand of the Prince of Syracuse, return empty-handed, down to the last, in which she has just given birth to a son.[4]   (K II 557, P II 536).

The image of the reliquary had been hinted at by Elstir, mentioning the sources of Fortuny's fabrics:

"You may, perhaps, before very long," Elstir informed her, "be able to gaze at the marvellous stuffs which they used to wear. One used only to be able to see them in the words of the Venetian painters, or very rarely among the treasures of old churches.   (K I 960, P I 898).

The reliquary implied by the 'trésors des églises' would be a literal receptacle, preserving a precious relic by wrapping it in precious material, and thus accidentally preserving the artistic motif in a way parallel to its preservation in a Carpaccio painting. In the *Côté de Guermantes* conceit we now find the whole procession of the *Sant' Orsola* sequence, in a series of tableaux echoing the paintings. The arrival of the ambassadors where the princess is offstage in simple indoor clothing,[5] the betrothal, the departure of the ambassadors, are all elided and scrambled among the Guermantes reminiscences. Each separate painting of the Carpaccio sequence is in its own right a triptych where the central panel is enclosed between the smaller narrative brackets of the left-hand and right-hand scene, and each third is enclosed not only within the frame of the narrative pauses, but also within the framework of a fictional series of pillars and arches, stairways and flagpoles. And the sequence as a whole is one massive reliquary, the separate paintings coming together to form a narrative sequence which is subsumed in miniature within each one of the separate paintings. The image of the reliquary is called forth by Proust's text: Marcel sees the names and memories of long-dead ancestors as relics preserved in the reliquary of a nostalgic discourse preserving the individual in the structure and context of the past:

Sometimes, rather than of a race, it was of a particular fact, of a date, that a name reminded me. [...]

Sometimes it was more than a simple relic that I saw. Better informed than his wife as to what their ancestors had been, M. de Guermantes had at his command memories which gave to his conversation a fine air of an ancient mansion, lacking in real masterpieces but still full of pictures, authentic, indifferent and majestic, which taken as a whole has an air of grandeur. [...] At once I was lost in contemplation of a reliquary such as Carpaccio or Memling used to paint. (K II 556–7, P II 536).

I need hardly point out that this process of embedding through evocation is an almost transparent projection of Proust's own discursive construction. The image of embedding is picked up again in a revealing reference to Balzac's habit of inserting real historical figures in cameo roles in the *Comédie humaine*:

(We see for other reasons in a gazetteer of the works of Balzac, where the most illustrious personages figure only to the extent of their connexion with the *Comédie Humaine*, Napoleon occupying a space considerably less than that allotted to Rastignac, and occupying that space solely because he once spoke to Mlle de Cinq-Cygne.) (K II 558, P II 537).

This gives a fair indication of the way in which real paintings by Carpaccio or apparently real dresses by Fortuny are keyed into Proust's text. Real paintings by Carpaccio, evoked by the real designer Fortuny, illustrate with their structures and motifs the concerns of Proust's fictitious painter Elstir, who introduces, explains and authenticates their models – whilst Proust of course is using their metaphorical and regressive structures and motifs to surreptitiously motivate Elstir's paintings and aesthetics. In addition, the whole process of structuring a work of art from the highly intricate cross-referencing of individual motifs is equated with the ability of the mind to process memory in similar fashion:

Thus the empty spaces of my memory were covered by degrees with names which in arranging, composing themselves in relation to one another, in linking themselves to one another by increasingly numerous connexions, resembled those finished works of art in which there is not one touch that is isolated, in which every part in turn receives from the rest a justification which it confers on them in turn. (K II 558, P II 537).

The reliquary theme reaches the acme of its structural complexity at the moment of the resurrection of the Carpaccio motif by Fortuny:

These Fortuny gowns, one of which I had seen Mme de Guermantes wearing, were those of which Elstir, when he told us about the magnificent garments of the women of Carpaccio's and Titian's day, had prophesied the imminent return from their ashes, as magnificent as of old, for everything must return in time, as it is written beneath the vaults of St Mark's, and proclaimed, as they drink from the urns of marble and jasper of the Byzantine capitals, by the birds which symbolise at once death and resurrection.

(K III 375–6, P III 368).

The first *mise en abîme* is the one overtly announced by Proust, the phoenix-like resurrection of Carpaccio's dresses in Fortuny's. This figure is of course superimposed on the earlier resurrection or preservation of the dresses themselves by the painter, and it creates in its turn a new figure where the dresses enclose an image of the painting which revived them:

Now even if these gowns were not those genuine antiques in which women today seem a little too got up in fancy dress [...] neither did they have the coldness of the artificial, the sham antique. Like the theatrical designs of Sert, Bakst and Benois, who at that moment were recreating in the Russian ballet the most cherished periods of art with the aid of works of art impregnated with their spirit and yet original, these Fortuny gowns, faithfully antique but markedly original, brought before the eye like a stage decor, and with an even greater evocative power since the decor was left to the imagination, that Venice saturated with oriental splendour where they would have been worn and of which they constituted, even more than a relic in the shrine of St. Mark, evocative as they were of the sunlight and the surrounding turbans, the fragmented, mysterious and complementary colour. (K III 376, P III 369).

The sense of this comparison is that the dresses should function through their general revival of images alluding to Venetian painting of the period, rather than by copying the historically exact dresses – they should be an image of an image, perhaps a metaphor of a metaphor.

The legend 'tout doit revenir' is actually nowhere written on the arches of St Mark's, but Proust is no doubt remembering and paraphrasing a famous remark of Ruskin in the 'St Mark's' chapter of *The Stones of Venice:*

Not in the wantonness of wealth, not in vain ministry to the desire of the eyes or the pride of life, were those marbles hewn into transparent strength, and those arches arrayed in the colours of the iris. There is a message written in the dyes of them, that once was written in blood; and a sound that echoes in their vaults, that one day shall fill the vault of heaven; – 'He shall return to do judgment and justice.' (Morris 97).[6]

Here is the idea of a resurrection – the resurrection of Christ – being in its turn preserved through the artistry of the coloured mosaic iconography. Proust's shorthand transcription turns Ruskin's insight into a more radically simplified textual mirroring: the legend 'tout doit revenir' is itself preserved in letters or icons, and they are symbolised by neighbouring peacocks which both exemplify the survival of beauty through art and simultaneously represent their perpetual resurrection as Christian symbols of eternal life being drunk from the eucharistic chalice. The birds also perform their own iconographic resurrection within Proust's text by reviving the brilliant peacock image of the stained-glass window at Combray, and by preparing the ground for the peacock-like napkin which will bring the sea flooding back into Marcel's Parisian life at the Guermantes' reception in *Le Temps retrouvé*.

But this whole process of textual, iconographic and spiritual resurrection in its turn is transfigured into the image of a reliquary:

these Fortuny gowns, faithfully antique but markedly original, brought before the eye like a stage decor, and with an even greater evocative power since the decor was left to the imagination, that Venice saturated with oriental splendour where they would have been worn and of which they constituted, even more than a relic in the shrine of St Mark, evocative as they were of the sunlight and the surrounding turbans, the fragmented, mysterious and complementary colour. Everything of those days had perished, but everything was being reborn, evoked and linked together by the splendour and the swarming life of the city, in the piecemeal reappearance of the still-surviving fabrics worn by the Doges' ladies.

(K III 376, P III 369).

Inside St Mark's is the treasury, inside the treasury is the reliquary, inside the reliquary is the relic preserved. Originally the paintings of Carpaccio captured and preserved fugitively fashionable oriental motifs; the Venetian paintings in question resuscitate the Orient. Carpaccio either travelled to Constantinople or was influenced by Gentile Bellini's trip[7] (which produced among other reports of Oriental art and fashion the portrait of Mahomet II in 1479, used by Swann when commenting on Bloch's features and by the narrator when commenting on Swann's jealousy) (K I 105, 386, P I 97, 355). There are authentic Middle-Eastern costumes in Carpaccio's *Patriarche di Grado* (now usually called *Guarigione d'un ossesso*), mentioned in *La Fugitive* (K III 662, P III 647), but also more overwhelmingly in Carpaccio's *San Giorgio* sequence.

The metaphor is striking enough – the sporadic appearance of Carpaccian motifs in Fortuny dresses being likened to the preservation of a relic in a reliquary. The justness of the imagery is reinforced by the fact that such a reliquary might well be decorated in reality by Carpaccio or a contemporary Venetian painter, that such a relic might well be wrested from the Orient by the piratical Venetian crusaders or merchants, and that such a reliquary, in the form of a miniature model of the church of St Sophia in Constantinople, could be enclosed in the treasury of St Mark's (which is a copy of it ...) – giving another vertiginous dimension to the *mise en abîme*.

But the 'piecemeal reappearance of the still-surviving fabrics worn by the Doges' ladies' (the resurrectional emotion being perhaps underlined by the rare moment of clumsiness in Proust's discordant tautology: 'reappearance'/'still-surviving' – *surgissement/survivant?*), taken in relation to the reliquary, has an even deeper thematic and structural motivation. If we turn to the writings of art-historian Emile Mâle, one of the major sources, with Ruskin, of Proust's religious and artistic knowledge, we can go further than Autret's

interesting identification of Proust's inspiration, concerning the preservation of the Oriental motif through western religious art, via
Venice:

These so-called symbols would often be carved after the design on a piece
of Persian fabric or an Arabian carpet [...] Our 13th-century sculptors
[...] copied the figures in the Byzantine carpets brought to France by the
merchants of Venice [...] We shall see that designs from Persian, Byzantine
and Arabian fabric were copied to an equal extent, and that it is from Oriental
cloth that our artists borrowed the monsters which they carved on their
capitals.

(Autret 150/Mâle, *L'Art religieux du XIIIe siècle en France*, 1898, pp. 68–9).[8]

For there is in Mâle a more interesting idea than the simple copying
and transmission of an Oriental motif. The reliquary is already
precious, already a work of art. It contains within it a material
which is also precious, also a work of art. But the material which
contains the precious relic, subsumes it as it were into its fabric,
becoming a relic in its turn, albeit a transcendentally informed, artistic relic:

One of the early customs of the church was to preserve the relics of its
saints in the most sumptuous fabrics: no covering could be too splendid
for these sacred remains. Thus it is that some extremely ancient pieces of
cloth have survived into modern times because they were enclosed within
reliquaries. They were later removed and are now preserved in the treasure-
rooms of our churches [...]. Only shreds remain, but they provide an abbre-
viated history of this decorative art over a period of seven or eight centuries.
(*La Revue de Paris*, 1921, pp. 712–13; Mâle, *L'Art religieux du XIIe siècle
en France*, published in book form after Proust's death in 1922, but this
and other extracts appeared in *La Revue de Paris* in 1921.)[9]

I believe that Proust has developed an insight of Mâle's (as to the
accidental transmission of art through religious practice) and used
it as the basis of his idea that a decorative fabric (the Fortuny dress)
may serve as the vehicle of preservation of artistic genius (the Carpaccio painting) which in its turn transformed a merely decorative/func-
tional/religious matter (certain Oriental costumes and motifs) into
the preservative and transcendental medium of art, by a process
of *mise en abîme* whereby the relations of content and form are
inverted.

The birds on Proust's Fortuny dresses are not only a metaphor for revival, they are also the substance of that revival; and while the narrator watches them, the symbolic birds become transmuted into the very stuff of art, the glass and gold of the stained-glass window and the reliquary:

The Fortuny gown which Albertine was wearing that evening seemed to me the tempting phantom of that invisible Venice. It was covered with Arab ornamentation, like the Venetian palaces hidden like sultan's wives behind a screen of pierced stone, like the bindings in the Ambrosian Library, like the columns from which the oriental birds that symbolised alternatively life and death were repeated in the shimmering fabric, of an intense blue which, as my eyes drew nearer, turned into a malleable gold by those same transmutations which, before an advancing gondola, change into gleaming metal the azure of the Grand Canal. (K III 401, P III 394).

As he watches the motif's repetition, he finds himself studying the patterning of his own work, where instead of merely copying motifs (from Carpaccio or Fortuny or from any other Venetian or religious art) he revives and preserves them through fragmentation and transposition: in his work like Fortuny's and Carpaccio's, 'everything was being reborn [...] in the piecemeal reappearance of the still-surviving fabrics worn by the Doges' ladies' (K III 376, P III 369).

Mâle himself noted the Byzantine connection and the bird motif, particularly the two-headed eagle and the intertwined or symmetrically facing birds, at the heart of the process of artistic and spiritual transmission and preservation:

These magnificent pieces of cloth, which were displayed everywhere in church and were even draped over the shoulders of the priest at the altar could not fail to excite the artists' imagination. The artist is the man whose faculty of admiration is more highly developed than that of his fellows. [...] Many Arabian fabrics were decorated with beautiful birds placed symmetrically either side of a flowering stem. Sometimes the two birds are back-to-back, but with their heads turned back in an elegant gesture to face each other. There are just such birds in our own tradition [...]. Romanesque buildings constantly provide us with strange symbols laden with centuries of emotion; an abacus in the cloisters at Moissac is decorated with a series of two-headed eagles [...]. And now we are swept away in our imagination to the very cradle of the world, to ancient Chaldea. For it is in fact an extremely old Chaldean cylinder which first shows a two-headed eagle [...]. It is a great eagle, a sort of roc from the *Arabian Nights*, with each claw placed on the back of a lion [...]. How was this ancient Oriental symbol transmitted to us? Through designs on pieces of cloth, as usual. In the Cathedral of Sens there is a piece of fabric (although only a shred remains) which is decorated with two-headed eagles woven in yellow on a violet-purple background. It is a Byzantine fabric from the 9th or 10th century which no doubt reproduces an earlier Sassanid original [...]. It is no doubt from the Orient that this blazon comes. It was borrowed from Oriental fabrics, perhaps even from Moslem battle-standards. It is strange to realise that the Turkish fleet at the battle of Lepanto was faced with the vessels of Don Juan of Austria flying the ensign of the two-headed eagle which had in former times been borne on their own flags. The ancient eagle of Chaldea, which had once brought them victory, had now turned against them [...]. Thus it is in the distant Oriental past that we must seek the origins of our own decorative arts of the Middle Ages. Among the motifs which we find in our churches, we should not forget the graceful arabesque formed by two birds with intertwined necks: their long necks as they intertwine form a sort of caduceum [...]. In the whole of the Orient, indeed, we find animals with intertwined necks. We see them [...] painted on the frontispiece of an Armenian manuscript: there, the birds with their necks intertwined are two magnificent peacocks [...]. We have every reason to believe that they were transmitted from East to West, as usual, through Sassanid and Arabian fabrics [...]. Our Romanesque capitals sometimes show us two creatures so closely united that they have but one head for two bodies.   (Mâle, in *La Revue de Paris*, pp. 716–25).

Thus Albertine's dual eagle is set in its Venetian context, its ambiguity echoing that of Venice, facing both ways as importer of Oriental goods and ideas but exporter of Crusades and Imperialism: neatly summarised in La Serenissima's great but already anachronistic victory over the Turks at Lepanto. The facing or amorously intertwined peacocks which form the basic repertoire of Proust's Fortuny motifs, are there, as is the roc from the *Arabian Nights*.

I have been unable to trace any Fortuny dresses with a phoenix motif. One piece of material in the Fortuny museum sports a bird of vaguely peacock-like appearance. I have in my possession, however, a print of one of Fortuny's own archive photographs of one of his cloths with a magnificent series of two-headed eagles, copied from a Byzantine silk of the 11th or 12th century (negativo originale no. 3150). The birds have a strikingly peacock-like plumage.

11   Mariano Fortuny, Cloth designed after a twelth-century Byzantine
        original, Museo Fortuny, Venice (Photo M. Fortuny).

12   Mariano Fortuny, Cloth with facing birds, Museo Fortuny, Venice
                (Photo P. Collier).

Fortuny, like Mâle's Romanesque craftsman, was an admirer and a transcriber. Proust in *Le Temps retrouvé* makes no higher claim for his own art than for it to be a celebration of experience, and a translation of it. His invention of non-existent peacock motifs in Fortuny dresses is an example of this kind of inspired, admirative re-creation. Originality is achieved through a transposition or inversion of existing structures.

When Proust associates Albertine with Austria (making us think of the Hapsburg version of the two-headed eagle, a common Venetian motif since the Austrian occupation of Venice in the nineteenth century), he talks of an 'inversion of symbols' (K II 1157, P II 1119). And indeed, at a crucial stage in *La Fugitive* the whole process of regression and mirroring is itself inverted. At this point in his Venetian Odyssey Marcel catches sight in Carpaccio's *Patriarche di Grado* of the cloak of a 'Compagno della Calza'. This cloak was copied by (Proust's) Fortuny from the painting, and now the sight of the Carpaccio original revives the memory of the copy worn by Albertine, and thereby revives the dead Albertine for Marcel. The sight of the original Carpaccio (itself a transcendental inversion of precious motif and material) revives the Fortuny copy – which resurrects in its wake the body of Albertine that it shrouded. This moment of the resurrection of the resurrection is one of the most significant stages in Marcel's progress towards artistic and spiritual rebirth (K III 662, P III 647). It is a brilliant projection of the kind of *mise en abîme* intuited by Mâle, inverting tenor and vehicle.[10] Mâle explains how a military banner mistakenly takes on the aura of a religious relic, and how this pious motivation, however erroneous, enables it to survive as a work of art:

By a strange twist of fate we owe to a misunderstanding the preservation in the treasure-house of the church of Apt, in Provence, of a fine Moslem fabric, which is probably a flag. It has been known for some centuries as the Veil of St Ann, and protected carefully as a relic [...]. Thus at Apt we have what is doubtless a trophy looted from the Holy City [...]. This is the oldest memento extant in France of our crusaders' victories: but it is virtually unknown. (Mâle, op cit., p. 715).

It is not far-fetched to parallel this with Proust's own preference for the accidental and the erroneous in his theory of aesthetic resurrection in *Le Temps retrouvé*, whereby the selfish, bodily material of everyday living, rather than the transcendental goals pursued, becomes the material of artistic salvation. The Crusader who donated the Saracen banner to his local church in Apt was no more nor less materialist than Marcel, with his frenzied quest for love, gentility, fame or knowledge. Mâle parallels other of Proust's concerns in *La Fugitive* and *Le Temps retrouvé*. The quasi-accidental preservation of the precious artistic motif, along with the precious religious relic it was meant to protect, presents us with a model of *mise en abîme* like that of the Fortuny dress. The decorative material was intended to merely embellish and preserve the relic for posterity – in fact it acts as the fragile reliquary of the even more priceless material of artistic form; an eventual spiritual resurrection being prepared through its contingent, formal beauty:

Thus our stonecarvers did not always intend to instruct; most often they wished merely to decorate [...]. In Gaul, in Merovingian times, it was Oriental tapestries which provided the most magnificent decoration for the Christian basilicas. They were hung over doors and between pillars; they screened the sanctuary to make it impenetrable, like the Holy of Holies. They decorated the sarcophagi where the confessors and the martyrs lay buried [...]. The 6th century after Christ saw the rebirth of artistic forms which were three thousand years old. Doubtless they had never really died, but the reign of the Sassanids, which was an age of resurrection for Persia, gave them new life, and rejuvenated them.   (Mâle, op. cit., pp. 712–13).

We can imagine the impact that this imaginative piece of art history must have had on Proust, in the last year of his life, with much of the manuscript of *A la recherche du temps perdu* (including *La fugitive* and *Le temps retrouvé*) unpublished or unfinished, and the survival of Proust's name and art still uncertain. Mâle evokes the death of the bodily (through his references to the relic and the shroud) as if it were necessary for survival in artistic and spiritual forms. A similar attitude will become clear in *Le Temps retrouvé*.

For Mâle, these artistic forms are seen to be resurrected, phoenix-like, in terms of their very colours – those of a slow fire still burning amid the ashes of its apparent destruction:

The Sassanid tapestries, and the Byzantine tapestries which copy them, are woven in colours of gold and of fire; sometimes they are also the colour of ashes, but it is an ashen pink or an ashen blue, and their exquisite shades are enchanting. These are the fairy-lights of sunset dying away in the heavens when the sun has sunk from view. (Mâle, pp. 713–14).

Those colours (gold, blue, pink) are also the privileged colours of the Fortuny dresses (inspired by Carpaccio, who was inspired by the kind of Oriental model that Mâle mentions).

But perhaps the most powerful insight of Mâle's, in relation to Proust's aesthetic of *mise en abîme*, is the idea that the Oriental drapery and the Oriental carpet, used to decorate the plain window and plain floor of the Romanesque church, were then recreated, in an imitation of their borrowed decoration, to yet take on the more lasting, and paradoxically more original, form of the stained-glass window and the mosaic:

I am convinced, for instance, that the origins of the stained-glass window must be seen as an imitation of Oriental fabrics. It was customary in the Middle Ages, even as late as the 14th century, to cover windows with fabric. If in our mind's eye we draw a beautiful piece of Oriental fabric over the window of a Romanesque church we will create the image of a stained-glass window: there are the same background of bright purple or azure, the same circles within which the subject is inscribed, the same ornamental or dotted border around the outside of the circles, the same fronds deployed between the circles in order to fill in the empty spaces in the background [...]. Just such fabrics, drawn over the windows of the basilicas in Carolingian times, inspired our first painters on glass. It was not long before these beautiful Byzantine fabrics, where scenes from the gospel were woven within circles, tempted them to include in their windows representations of sacred history.

The Oriental carpet spread over the floor was often used as a model for the mosaic which formed the paving of the sanctuary. Nothing could be more natural than to make such copies: mosaics were in their way a carpet, but one which lasted longer than wool. This source of mosaic paving in the Roman period is often very easy to detect. (Mâle, op. cit., pp. 716–17).

The image of cloth stretched over a light to project an image of a stained-glass window may remind us how Marcel's imagination clothes an unreal image of Oriane de Guermantes with coloured light and forms from a stained-glass window in the church of St

Hilaire; and how the fabric of Fortuny's dresses is moulded against the resistant reality of Albertine's body, allowing Marcel's imagination to weave a glittering mosaic of fantasies based on Carpaccian pictures and Venetian motifs.

This inscription of narrative imagery into the welcoming shapes and intervals of the window also recalls the magic lantern shows of Marcel's childhood. The body of the hero, Golo of Brabant, envelops a door or door handle, miraculously ingesting the interfering matter that intrudes upon the artistic forms projected by the magic lantern on the bedroom walls, as if the building, not the slides, were transparent, and as if the hero, able to use his galloping rhythm to transmute the curtains into waves, could remodel the contours of his environment like an artist (K I 10, P I 10). But later, when the ageing narrator recalls this experience at the Guermantes', because he is struck by the strangely modified appearance of a former acquaintance, Argencourt, it is Time itself which projects its lantern upon the body, moulding its matter to suit a revelation of its own patterns: the individual at any one moment is only part of a shifting configuration of images, and, as he grows older, Time's vertebrae show up more clearly among the surface imagery (K III 964, P III 924). What is striking in these two references to the magic lantern, which both seem to develop a model close to that of Emile Mâle, is that the earlier reference suggests the power of art to restructure, while the later reference, made at a point when the narrator is about to despair, suggests that death is a more powerful artist. It is typical of the logic of Proust's book that ultimately it is the earlier, unexplained artistic model which will triumph, by the time that the structure of the whole book has ingested the various images and contours of transitory experience.

And the idea that domestic art (of the carpet) becomes preserved through artifice and imitation in the apparently more intractable medium of the stone mosaic, evokes the structuring power of the mental mosaic of Proust's anti-realistic art – which intuition is of course alluded to *en abîme* in the novel, not least through the projection of the colours and patterns of carvings of stained-glass windows onto the paving-stones of Venice or Combray.

Certain patterns in Mâle's thought are particularly close to Proust's. It is the fact that the material is hidden and forgotten and considered secondary that allows it to mature inside its container and then be revealed – like the experience of Marcel (when correctly understood) in *Le Temps retrouvé*. The container of the relic was contained in the casket. It is then removed and becomes contained within a vaster treasury, having itself become a more valuable and lasting relic. This kind of *mise en abîme* is fundamental to Proust's analysis of Fortuny and Carpaccio, but also to many parts of the *Recherche*: the celebrated description of the carafe in the river where the contained and container relationships between water and glass in the Vivonne are continuously reflected and transposed is an isolated example;[11] a wider, structural resonance is to be found in the setting within the text of a detailed and ramified description of a church, St Hilaire, which embedding will finally become reversed when it will be the text itself which becomes the cathedral – the book having evolved as it were from inside the architecture of Combray and its church. And perhaps we should not forget that Mâle rehabilitates the profane, materialistic weaver, and the collector, of pretty patterns, much as Proust sets his derivative dress-designer, Fortuny, at the apex of creativity. And we think above all of Proust's most writerly metaphor for his work (the notorious cathedral metaphor does not come so close to the act of writing), when in *Le Temps retrouvé* he compares his labour to that of Françoise making a dress. We have seen that Fortuny's dresses are works of art – now we see the construction of the work of art in terms of a dressmaker's humble craftsmanship:

I should work beside her and in a way almost as she worked herself (or at least as she had worked in the past, for now, with the onset of old age, she had almost lost her sight) and, pinning here and there an extra page, I should construct my book, I dare not say ambitiously like a cathedral, but quite simply like a dress. [...]

These 'paperies,' as Françoise called the pages of my writing, it was my habit to stick together with paste, and sometimes in this process they became torn. But Françoise then would be able to come to my help, by consolidating them just as she stitched patches on to the worn parts of her dresses or as, on the kitchen window, while waiting for the glazier as I was waiting for the printer, she used to paste a piece of newspaper where a pane of glass had been broken. And she would say to me, pointing to my note-books as though they were worm-eaten wood or a piece of stuff which the moth had got into: "Look, it's all eaten away, isn't that dreadful! There's nothing left of this bit of page, it's been torn to ribbons," and examining it with a tailor's eye she would go on: "I don't think I shall be able to mend this one, it's finished and done for. A pity, perhaps it has your best ideas. You know what they say at Combray: there isn't a furrier who knows as much about furs as the moth, they always get into the best ones." (K III 1090–1, P III 1033–4).

As the religiously useful and precious material protecting the relic triumphs in tatters through the preservation of its own aesthetic motif, so Françoise sees that shreds of paper, as their material rots, take on a fragile, formal beauty, that of lace. The final fitting of the stained-glass window (the publishing of the work) is a mechanical, official action: the real work of shoring up the text against the drafts of time is done with card. Proust's whole textual composition is also discovered in this witty passage, his lateral or internal patchwork expansion, his strengthening of theme through the repetition of used motifs. And also the resurrection theme: the thought is preserved on paper, the paper rots and tears, the writer labours to patch and repair and increase as time wears and tears and eats away – until finally the published work will transcend and subsume the limitations of the paper pattern and express the mosaic of the original thought.

8

Born again: Marcel's mosaic

It is possible to imitate with square little pieces of glass, though not very exactly, either the Good or the Bad.

Goethe

Elle rêve d'un autre temps où la même chose qui va se produire se produirait différemment. Autrement. Mille fois. Partout. Ailleurs. Entre d'autres, des milliers qui, de même que nous, rêvent de ce temps, obligatoirement. Ce rêve me contamine.

Marguerite Duras

When Marcel enters the Baptistery of St Mark's Basilica in Venice, the reader may justifiably expect some exceptional spiritual reverberation to awaken the text of *A la recherche du temps perdu*, so long has Marcel waited to penetrate the inner sanctum of his holy city. Yet most critics have ignored the crucial importance of this passage (K III 660–1, P III 645–6).[1]

Louis Bolle however notes that the appearance of St Mark's and the Campanile are prefigured by the appearances of the church and steeple of St Hilaire: 'Indeed the campanile *recapitulates* all the other steeples and reveals the answers to their respective riddles', as its golden angel announces a new age *'where time is regained or redeemed,* where what was hidden is brought out and made manifest'. Bolle cites the phoenix motif, the Carpaccian designs of Fortuny's dresses, the motto 'tout doit revenir'. [2]

But there is a new dimension to Proust's symbolism as Marcel enters the Baptistery:

My mother and I would enter the baptistery, treading underfoot the marble and glass mosaics of the paving, in front of us the wide arcades whose curved pink surfaces have been slightly warped by time, thus giving the church, wherever the freshness of this colouring has been preserved, the appearance of having been built of a soft and malleable substance like the wax in a giant honeycomb, and, where time has shrivelled and hardened the material and artists have embellished it with gold tracery, of being the precious binding, in the finest Cordoba leather, of the colossal Gospel of Venice. Seeing that I needed to spend some time in front of the mosaics representing the Baptism of Christ, and feeling the icy coolness that pervaded the baptistery, my mother threw a shawl over my shoulders. [...] A time has now come when, remembering the baptistery of St Mark's – contemplating the waters of the Jordan in which St John immerses Christ, while the gondola awaited us at the landing-stage of the Piazzetta – it is no longer a matter of indifference to me that, beside me in that cool penumbra, there should have been a woman draped in her mourning with the respectful and enthusiastic fervour of the old woman in Carpaccio's *St Ursula* in the Accademia, and that that woman, with her red cheeks and sad eyes and in her black veils, whom nothing can ever remove from that softly lit sanctuary of St Mark's where I am always sure to find her because she has her place reserved there as immutably as a mosaic, should be my mother.

(K III 660–1, P III 646).

Gérard Genette notes the baptismal analogies at work: the mosaics depict baptism, within the site of the baptistry devoted to the function of baptism, and the Jordan mosaic is echoed by the Venetian waters outside, while the cold air falls like baptismal water. He also notes the metonymic connections with works of art: the mother resembling one in Carpaccio's painting, as well as resembling a mosaic figure, presumably the mother of Christ.[3]

Jean-Pierre Richard links the theme of baptism more strongly with the theme of resuscitation, recalling the symbolism of the nativity and baptism. He sees Marcel's mother in the Baptistery as a Virgin-Mary figure. He sees the importance of the fact that the later Guermantes'-paving-stone experience will revive the feeling of walking on the Baptistery floor, and that the church has become a gospel[4] (Ruskin of course had already called St Mark's 'the Temple-Book').[5] Richard notes that if Marcel's mother resembles the mother of Christ, then Marcel is very much a Christ-like, baptised and redeemed figure. Richard notes that, since Marcel has taken his copy of Ruskin into the Baptistery, Ruskin appears as the presiding genius behind the symbolic presence of St John the Baptist.[6] Richard also sees that the mosaics of the Baptistery may adumbrate the composition of Marcel's eventual and Proust's actual work.[7]

The significance of the passage has thus been indicated to a certain extent at least by these critics. Bearing in mind my own exploration of the Venetian theme in *La Recherche* as a whole, it should now be possible to get to the heart of its real functions and its fundamental meaning.

The connotations of baptism, and of the Evangelist's message, long dormant in the culturally saturated names 'baptistery' and 'St Mark's' (which seemed to indicate an artistic space rather than a spiritual topos), retrieve their Christian gloss, and Proust's text becomes heavily charged with iconographic and symbolic representations of baptism and the gospel. Literally, the mosaics in the Baptistery document the baptism of Christ by John the Baptist, and the Baptistery is the part of the church used for baptism, but metaphorically the whole church appears metamorphosed into a gilded binding for the 'gospel' of Venice ('the precious binding, in the finest Cordoba leather, of the colossal Gospel of Venice'), the air is described in terms of coldness and liquidity which evoke a dousing in icy baptismal waters ('the icy coldness that poured into the baptistery'), and the mother drapes her son with her shawl in a gesture which is not merely protective, but also recalls the customary presentation of the child to be christened in a shawl ('my mother threw a shawl over my shoulders'). Marcel's mature persona, the narrator, involves Marcel and his mother further in these baptismal connotations by a series of *mises en abîme*. John's baptism of Christ in the Jordan is telescoped into the arrival of mother and son at the Baptistery by gondola.

The impressionistic geography and its repetitive syntax: ('remembering the baptistery of St Mark's – contemplating the waters of the Jordan'), and the shifting pronominal reference ('St Mark's [...] St John [...] Christ [...] us [...] me') strengthen the parallel, so that the reader is invited to visualise the canals of Venice as the waters of the Jordan, leading the chosen couple to some superior goal.

The reader should no doubt remember Marcel's impression that when in a gondola he is following the mysterious guidance of a ray of light:

My gondola followed the course of the small canals; like the mysterious hand of a genie leading me through the maze of this oriental city, they seemed, as I advanced, to be cutting a path for me through the heart of a crowded quarter which they bisected, barely parting, with a slender furrow arbitrarily traced, the tall houses with their tiny Moorish windows; and as though the magic guide had been holding a candle in his hand and were lighting the way for me, they kept casting ahead of them a ray of sunlight for which they cleared a route.   (K III 641, P III 627).

This is rather reminiscent of a passage in *The Stones of Venice* where the figure of the Doge Andrea Dandolo (responsible for the mosaic decoration of St Mark's Baptistery, and buried symbolically at the heart of his own creation) is espied, immortalised in stone, as it were sleeping in his bedroom:

[...] a small figure of the Baptist standing above it in a single ray of light that glances across the narrow room, dying as it falls from a window high in the wall, and the first thing that it strikes, and the only thing that it strikes brightly, is a tomb. We hardly know if it be a tomb indeed; for it is like a narrow couch set beside the window [...] so that it might seem [...] to have been drawn towards the window, that the sleeper might be awakened early.   (Tr. Ed., pp. 105–6).

John the Baptist watches over the immortalised Andrea Dandolo: but the same scene would very well describe the genius of Ruskin presiding over the hero at this stage in his quest – burying one self, resuscitating another, and preparing to live on for ever in the mosaic of the work of art crystallising the mosaic of his life. I shall return to this parallel later. The whole topos of the motionless sleeper watching at the heart of his petrified creation is of course prepared right at the start of the *Recherche*, with its creator caught in his dream thought of falling asleep, and becoming a church; the while replacing the flickering flame of his bedside candle with the brighter blaze of his inner vision:

For a long time I used to go to bed early. Sometimes, when I had put out my candle, my eyes would close so quickly that I had not even time to say to myself: "I'm falling asleep." And half an hour later the thought that it was time to go to sleep would awaken me; I would make as if to put away the book which I imagined was still in my hands, and to blow out the light; I had gone on thinking, while I was asleep, about what I had just been reading, but these thoughts had taken a rather peculiar turn; it seemed to me that I myself was the immediate subject of my book: a church, a quartet, the rivalry between François I and Charles V.   (K13, P14).

In Combray the bedroom candle and bedtime book light the way into the inner reconstruction of the self, whereas in Venice it is a genie from the *Arabian Nights*, our archetypal self-generating narrative, that appears to lead our hero by candlelight into a dream-like reality, as he walks into a real-life, labyrinthine work of art. One thinks of course of Marcel's Carpaccian heroine, St Ursula, in the *Sogno di Sant' Orsola*, asleep but dreaming the angel who delivers her message, with Ursula's open book (bracketed between an unlit candle and a stopped hourglass) and the angel's poised quill pointing the paradoxical narrative power of the passive dreamer's mental structuring. For although Venice is to be the setting for a radical reordering of Marcel's life in terms of desire, memory and art, it is through art that the experiences of desire and memory are reworked. The Basilica of St Mark's refigures St Hilaire, the *Arabian Nights* reformulate the world of the boy who first travelled in the mind by courtesy of *François le Champi*, Giotto's figure of Envy rephrases the dream thought of the sleeper who opens the *Recherche*.

Venice has long been for the narrator a source of ideal and inspiration. Artistically, it has been the privileged home or source of paintings by Titian (procured by Marcel's grandmother), by Giotto in nearby Padua (proffered by Swann), by Carpaccio and Bellini. Emotionally, Venice has seemed to hold out a promise of erotic liberation; but both because of the fear that his aesthetic experience might be lessened by her presence, and because the erotic experience might be curtailed, Marcel has felt that he could not visit Venice with Albertine, although he has used her as a mannequin to help mirror his Venetian fantasies, figured in her Fortuny dresses. Albertine's death makes the Venetian trip possible. And indeed, on arrival, Marcel visits the Carpaccios in the Accademia, the Giottos in Padua, the mosaics in St Mark's. He tours the city in search of compliant working girls whenever he can get away from his mother, and he risks an outrageous affront to her by refusing to follow her to catch the train back to Paris, because he hopes to await the arrival in Venice of the notoriously promiscuous maid of the baronne Putbus.

The mutual interdiction linking Venice and Albertine is also positive, however. It would appear to offer Marcel a solution to the problem which Swann was unable to resolve with Odette, the problem of reconciling artistic work with erotic passion. Swann finds that love occupies every waking moment, and later, when he is no longer in love with Odette, it is marriage to her which obliges him to squander his aesthetic insights on trival small talk. Marcel however preserves his creative capital partly by trying to endow Albertine with his own aesthetic perceptions,[8] partly by refusing to take her with him to his Venetian shrine. His arrival in Venice is nonetheless at first disturbed by internal stirrings of a still-remembered Albertine. The telegram in which she appears to announce her survival and her marital intentions makes Marcel at last realise that the prospect of living with her leaves him indifferent; only at this moment does she become effectively dead for him. His love for her, which survived her death, is buried ('I had finally ceased to love Albertine') (K III 659, P III 644), and his age-old love for his mother returns to the centre of the stage. Since he fell morally in her eyes as a small boy unable to forego his goodnight kiss in the presence of his rival, Swann, and since he incurred her disapproval by living in sin with Albertine, she did not appear central to Marcel's drama. Marcel had even replaced his dependency on her goodnight kiss with a dependency on that of Albertine:

It was a soothing power the like of which I had not experienced since the evenings at Combray long ago when my mother, stooping over my bed, brought me repose in a kiss. (K III 71, P III 77).

But now, despite the recent loss of her own mother (which makes her and Marcel, who has lost his mistress, process in parallel mourning) Marcel's mother appears to view him with renewed favour, casting passionate smiles in his direction. But Albertine herself was not without a spiritual dimension. She appeared to preside over renderings of Vinteuil's music on the pianola like some painted wooden angel (a second-degree spiral of artistic experience worthy of the grandmother's engravings of Titian):

her dark, curling hair, presenting different conformations whenever she turned to ask me what she was to play next, now a splendid wing, sharp at the tip, broad at the base, black, feathered and triangular, now massing the contours of its curls in a powerful and varied chain, full of crests, of watersheds, of precipices, with its soft, creamy texture, so rich and so multiple, seeming to exceed the variety that nature habitually achieves and to correspond rather to the desire of a sculptor who accumulates difficulties in order to emphasise the suppleness, the vibrancy, the fullness, the vitality of his creation, brought out more strongly, by interrupting in order to cover it, the animated curve and, as it were, the rotation of the smooth, roseate face, with its glazed matt texture as of painted wood.

(K III 390, P III 383).

Yet her spirituality is already more than a superficial resemblance to a painted wooden sculpture, it is constituted by her ability to reconstitute in Marcel though aesthetic means the spiritual itinerary of memory, however erotic the form of the knowledge appears to be at this stage:

Just as the volume of that angel musician was constituted by the multiple journeys between the different points in the past which the memory of her occupied within me and the different signs, from the purely visual to the innermost sensations of my being, which helped me to descend into the intimacy of hers, so the music that she played had also a volume, produced by the unequal visibility of the different phrases, according as I had more or less succeeded in throwing light on them and joining up the lines of the seemingly nebulous structure. (K III 379, P III 372).

The spiritualisation of the flesh is signalled in Proust's language as Marcel offers his love to Albertine like 'a votive offering' (K III 71, P III 76), and feels as it were absolved by her for his emotional sin of doubting her sexual fidelity: 'I would deposit my doubts in her, hand them over for her to relieve me of them, with the abnegation of a worshipper uttering a prayer.' (K III 71, P III 77). The sanctuary of her room appeared transformed into something like a crib, whilst her own flesh was perceived as similar to the body of Christ:

And, by contrast with all this relief, by the harmony also which united them with her, who had adapted her attitude to their form and purpose, the pianola which half concealed her like an organ-case, the bookcase, the whole of that corner of the room, seemed to be reduced to the dimensions of a lighted sanctuary, the shrine of this angel musician, a work of art which, presently, by a charming magic, was to detach itself from its niche and offer to my kisses its precious, rose-pink substance.

(K III 390, P III 383).

In a manuscript variant her tongue even became a very profane host:

Incomparable as were those two kisses of peace, Albertine slipped into my mouth, in making me the gift of her tongue, as it were a gift of the Holy Ghost, conveyed to me a viaticum, left me with a provision of tranquillity almost as precious as when my mother in the evening at Combray used to lay her lips upon my forehead. (K III 72, P III 1070).

In Marcel's memory, in *La fugitive*, the angelic and the erotic are indissolubly linked:

I could see Albertine now, seated at her pianola, pink-faced beneath her dark hair; I could feel against my lips, which she would try to part, her tongue, her maternal, incomestible, nutritious, hallowed tongue, whose strange moist warmth, even when she merely ran it over the surface of my neck or my stomach, gave to those caresses of hers, superficial but somehow administered by the inside of her flesh, externalised like a piece of material reversed to show its lining, as it were the mysterious sweetness of a penetration. (K III 507–8, P III 497–8).

Again, the maternal, incestuous aspect of the kiss is tightly linked with the blasphemously religious. But it is the *artistic* figure of the *pianist* which sanctifies desire, mediated through the image of the erotic déshabillé and aesthetic form of the exposed lining of the dressing-gown, evoked here metonymically and surreptitiously by the erotic ambiguity of the mucous membranes implicated in erotic play, reinforcing the Carpaccian theme both through the more formal framing of the act of erotic undressing and through the metaphor of the close interfacing of the material and the flesh, the body and the message. Already in *La prisonnière*, the transformation of the profane cyclist from Balbec into the angelic musician, using for the pianola the same movement of her hands and feet as for the bicycle, is at least partly ascribed to the creative intervention of the artistic Marcel, using the Carpaccian dress as a medium:

Her shapely legs, which on the first day I had with good reason imagined as having manipulated throughout her girlhood the pedals of a bicycle, now rose and fell alternately upon those of the pianola, upon which Albertine, who had acquired an elegance which made me feel her more my own, because it was from myself that it came, pressed her shoes of cloth of gold. Her fingers, at one time accustomed to handle-bars, now rested upon the keys like those of a St Cecilia. (K III 389, P III 382).

Now these substitutes for maternal love are unnecessary, as Marcel's mother is given a higher spiritual resonance, and his own erotic activities are divested of their romance. The mother's mourning appears to be associated with the son rather than with the grand mother, and is associated with the dignity both of great art and of Christian martyrdom, as she reenacts a Carpaccian figure:

beside me [...] a woman draped in her mourning with the respectful and enthusiastic fervour of the old woman in Carpaccio's *St Ursula* in the Accademia, [...] my mother.   (K III 661, P III 646).

Indeed, in Carpaccio's *Martirio e funerali di Sant' Orsola* it does look like a mother figure mourning yet adoring a daughter just sacrificed and sanctified.[9] Ultimately, the borrowed illumination of St Ursula's martyrdom, the holy setting of the Basilica, and the neighbouring election of Christ by the Holy Spirit, make her figure take on a role similar to that of Mary, mother of Jesus.

The implied death and rebirth of the hero function on various levels. The mother could be mourning his lost innocence (in connection with either Albertine or the Venetian philandering, and the reference to a violated and sacrificed *daughter* helps to add a further note of sexual ambiguity),[10] as the Carpaccian mother bewails the rape and murder of Ursula and her virgin companions, or even his lost opportunity of marriage (in parallel again with Ursula who was on her way to get married in Britain).[11] But it is most tempting to feel that she is praying for his spiritual and artistic soul to be reborn as an artist.[12] The reader who knows the mosaics of the Baptistery is likely to feel that the sad, dark, veiled figure is very akin to that of Mary, severely cloaked in dark blue and holding an oldish infant on her knees whilst being addressed by a trumpeting angel, portrayed on the Baptistery roof. The weeping Madonna figure of the mosaics of Torcello cathedral, admirably described by Ruskin in *The Stones of Venice*, also comes to mind.[13] Both the angel of the Campanile and the angel of the Baptistery mosaic are blasting on trumpets – the symbol seems to neatly fit the Annunciation and the Last Judgement, the raising of the dead and the spiritual rebirth. In the mosaics in the Baptistery and Torcello cathedral, and in fact in every similar icon in Venice, 'Maria Regina' is signalled by the presence alongside the face of the mother of Christ of the Greek initials 'MP'. Marcel Proust, who studied the mosaic inscriptions of the Baptistery Ruskin in hand in order to check on the accuracy of his transcriptions, is unlikely to have missed the analogy.[14]

There is another dark, sad figure, but in bronze, shrouded as much as draped, standing on the massive bronze lid of the font. If we remember that Albertine, on Marcel's arrival in Venice, was struggling inside the 'piombi' or leaded prison of his unconscious mind, as if still alive within him but repressed by his conscious thoughts, we notice that the violent image of the prisoner struggling to push back the heavy lid of the notorious dungeons of St Mark's actually fits rather better the damp, basement dungeons of the same place, known as the 'pozzi', or wells. The font of the Baptistery with its enormous bronze lid is very like a well, which is hardly surprising in view of the similar function of the two containers, and in view of the fact that the architect of the font, Sansovino, was also the architect of some noted Venetian wells, as we have seen ...

The figure of Albertine is closely associated with that of memory:

Sometimes at dusk as I returned to the hotel I felt that the Albertine of long ago, invisible to my eyes, was nevertheless enclosed within me as in the *Piombi* of an inner Venice, the tight lid of which some incident occasionally lifted to give me a glimpse of that past. (K III 654, P III 639).

The heavy bronze figure standing on the lid and keeping Albertine/ memory trapped in the well could stand equally well for Marcel himself, for John the Baptist/John Ruskin in the name of religion or art, or for Marcel's mother.[15] And Proust hints at the redemptive power of memory and of narrative when he says that a phrase in a letter, reminding him of forgotten experience by accident, can act as the 'Open Sesame' of the *Arabian Nights*:

Thus for instance one evening a letter from my stockbroker reopened for me for an instant the gates of the prison in which Albertine dwelt within me, alive, but so remote, so profoundly buried that she remained inaccessible to me [...] And these words which had never recurred to my mind acted like an "Open sesame!" upon the hinges of the prison door.[16]

(K III 654, 655, P III 639, 641).

Yet the force of the allusion is that Albertine has at last been laid to rest in his memory, after the exorcistical false alarm of the telegram ('this love [...] had ended too [...] by succumbing [...] to the general law of oblivion') (K III 659, P III 644). But as Albertine falls into the 'oubliettes' as it were, memory simultaneously enshrines and conserves the image of his mother.[17]

Marcel remembers his previous denial that any emotional empathy was operative in the shared experience of reacting to a work of art:

When I was with Albertine at Balbec, I felt that she was revealing one of those insubstantial illusions which clutter the minds of so many people who do not think clearly, when she used to speak of the pleasure – to my mind baseless – that she would derive from seeing works of art with me. (K III 661, P III 646).

But now that the partner in the artistic experience (of contemplating the mosaics) is his mother and not Albertine, the purified emotional link enables him to recognise the validity of the notion, thereby, by implication, purifying and reinstating Albertine at the same time as consecrating the mother as a medium for heightened spiritual and artistic experience. As this skin of false consciousness is cast, there is not only an intellectual recognition of the truth, but an actual operation of its effect, as memory, enshrined in art, conserves the image of the mother participating in his artistic reflections (K III 661, P III 646). The mother becomes part of the evangelical mosaic, but not so much at the fleeting moment of perception of the mosaics as in the eternal sanctuary of memory. It is not quite yet the full-blown theory of involuntary memory which will erupt when, later in Paris, Marcel trips over the uneven pavement at the Guermantes' but it is a significant step forward from the steeples and the madeleine cake, which provoked unexplained pleasure in the presence of art and memory. In this new experience Marcel's memory of his mother provides her with a permanence and a stability which most of the fluctuating inhabitants of the remembered Combray seem to lack, a setting in stone which takes on the jewel-like beauty of the mosaic and the religious dignity of the mausoleum or statue, and this memory for the first time in the *Recherche* is operated from the viewpoint of the narrator's absolute present, rather than from the viewpoint of some still unenlightened seeker: it is his dutiful contemplation of the surrounding art which saves her, as he preserves her in the sanctuary of memory. And the eternisation of this newly purified love is due partly to her charitable, maternal sacrifice, draping him in her shawl amid the cold, baptismal dampness; partly to the son's participation in an act of artistic labour and intuition (the prolonged Ruskinian contemplation):[18]

I went up to my room to get ready to go out with my mother and to collect the notebooks in which I would take notes for some work I was doing on Ruskin. [...] I needed to spend some time in front of the mosaics.

(K III 660–1, P III 645–6).

Very soon after his visit to the Baptistery with his mother Marcel will experience a sudden revival of a memory of a Fortuny dress and Albertine with it, on seeing Carpaccio's *Patriarche di Grado* from which the dress was copied. This resuscitation too brings a strangely mixed emotion: 'I was overcome for a few moments by a vague feeling of desire and melancholy' (K III 662, P III 647), reminiscent of his mixed feelings when writing about the steeples of Martinville. In the Baptistery itself one major difference explaining the greater feeling of happiness is that the mother herself becomes one with the works of art around her, adopting the gestures of the depicted Virgin; another is that the son is working determinedly at his artistic production. Faced with a pleasurable intuition when observing the steeples, he persevered at writing about what he saw. Here it is the previously decided act of writing (entering the Baptistery with his notebooks) that creates the pleasurable intuition. The author is creating a permanent artistic record out of a moment of authentic emotion. But this time there is a crucial distinction. When he recorded his observation of the steeples, the scene observed remained distinct from his own feelings; as far as he was aware he was recording some reality secreted by the steeples.[19] Now the scene not only includes him and his mother and the memory of Albertine, but it takes on meaning through their association with the various artistic motifs they appear to enact: the nativity, the baptism, the crucifixion, the pietà, the resurrection. The suddenly stabilised figures of Albertine and the mother for instance are very like those of the dignified Virgin Mary and the repentant, rehabilitated Mary Magdalene so often depicted in Western art with the dead Christ.

A certain Marcel has to die, the Marcel attached to Albertine, and another Marcel has to be born, the artistic Marcel. He has already summarised the message of St Mark's as 'tout doit revenir', which carefully elides the difference between the revival of past experience, and spiritual transcendence and salvation. We have noted how the Venetian theme runs through the novel, and how *La Prisonnière* and *La Fugitive* are constantly shimmering with the reflected promise of resurrection through the forms of the phoenix, the peacock, the Fortuny dress and the Carpaccio painting. Here Marcel turns his very deepest emotional experience, his relationship with Albertine and with his mother, into a reenactment of the timeless artworks of St Mark's. But he also hints that the real artistry lies in the artform of memory, seen as a mosaic. And, finally, Proust suggests by the integration of his mother's figure into the Carpaccio sequence which secreted the survival of the precious past through art, and the mosaic structure which he both studies and remembers, that she too will be saved by means of transcendental artistry, and that this time it is Marcel rather than Fortuny who will operate the revival, and will thereby himself survive.[20] Those familiar with the mosaics of St Mark's or Torcello or virtually any Venetian church will remember now perhaps that the colours of the Virgin Mary's garment are invariably deep blue, with a gold border – the most typical colours of the Fortuny dresses described – or created – by Proust.[21]

The resurrection, apparently triggered by Marcel's rather casually felt creative drive, effects a new translation of love and of artistic pleasure. The love for Albertine, which survived her death, is buried, and the purified love for the mother is enthroned.[22] This resurrection, less spectacular than those of the madeleine or the paving stone, is equally significant and possibly more moving. Throughout the stay in Venice, Combray has been coming back in patches: the artistic city triggers images and sensations within Marcel, whilst simultaneously recreating them in artistic form:

I received there impressions analogous to those which I had felt so often
in the past at Combray, but transposed into a wholly different and far richer
key. When, at ten o'clock in the morning, my shutters were thrown open,
I saw blazing there, instead of the gleaming black marble into which the
slates of Saint-Hilaire used to turn, the golden angel on the campanile of
St Mark's.   (K III 637, P III 623).

In their contact with the Venetian gold, the slates of Combray have
become marble, as if they were prints developed from negatives,
or as if an original were restored in place of a black and white reproduction. But there is also another example at this point of Proust's
textualisation of Mâle's idea that French cathedrals encapsulate
Byzantine art forms. If Combray contains the seeds of Venice, it
is particularly through the generative power of its church's architecture, and the awakening gaze of the artistic observer, increasingly
able to admire form, and to restructure his previous experience
accordingly.

In fact, Combray had prepared for Venice in advance through such
detail. The tombstones lining the floor of the Eglise St Hilaire had
become so worn and blurred with the passage of feet and time that
they were virtually liquefied, looking forward to the watery framework of the arrival at St Mark's; and the image Proust used, of
honey overflowing the defining contours of the comb, no doubt
looked forward to the Venetian paving and to the mosaic figure
itself, restructuring and reordering writing:

time had softened them and made them flow like honey beyond their regular
margins, here oozing out in a golden stream, washing from its place a
florid Gothic capital, drowning the white violets of the marble floor, and
elsewhere reabsorbed into their limits, contracting still further a crabbed
Latin inscription, bringing a fresh touch of fantasy into the arrangement
of its curtailed characters, closing together two letters of some word of
which the rest were disproportionately distended.   (K I 63–4, P I 59).

in front of us the wide arcades whose curved pink surfaces have been slightly
warped by time, thus giving the church, wherever the freshness of this
colouring has been preserved, the appearance of having been built of a
soft and malleable substance like the wax in a giant honeycomb.

(K III 661, P III 646).

There is also a more simple preparation for the revival of St Hilaire in St Mark's, in the uneven paving stones of 'a floor in which there are not two slabs on the same level' (K I 112, P I 103); which uneven stone is mentioned in general terms in relation to the above-mentioned 'arcades whose curved pink surfaces have been slightly warped by time'; and which recur explicitly *in memory* outside the Guermantes' residence:

as I moved sharply backwards I tripped against the irregular paving-stones in front of the coach-house. And at the moment when, recovering my balance, I put my foot on a stone which was slightly lower than its neighbour, all my discouragement vanished [...] And almost at once I recognised the vision: it was Venice, of which my efforts to describe it and the supposed snapshots taken by my memory had never told me anything, but which the sensation which I had once experienced as I stood upon two uneven stones in the baptistery of St Mark's had, recurring a moment ago, restored to me complete with all the other sensations linked on that day to that particular sensation, all of which had been waiting in their place – from which with imperious suddenness a chance happening had caused them to emerge – in the series of forgotten days.   (K III 898–900, P III 866–7).

The overlapping stones transgressing their contours are themselves a beautiful *mise en abîme* of the overlap of experience which they figure, a *mise en abîme* emphasised by the echo of 'propre équarissure' [regular margins] in 'mal équarris' [irregular].

Another significant overlap is in the person of Théodore, the sacristan – 'Theodore has a little book he lends people that tells the whole story' (K I 114, P I 105). The little book explaining the Eglise St Hilaire could be seen as prefiguring the work by Ruskin which Marcel takes into the Baptistery of St Mark's to help him understand the mosaics, which itself is a *mise en abîme* of the figure of Christ looming with his larger Book in his hand everywhere in the mosaics of St Mark's. The revival is all the more neatly orchestrated for St Theodore having been the patron saint of Venice, until his replacement by St Mark (in itself an echo of a kind of Old Testament/New Testament structure which we see occurring in the revival of Marcel himself). In St Mark's square St Theodore is sculpted standing over his vanquished dragon on a column alongside the one on which stalks Mark's winged, evangelical lion.[23] And Theodore's sister, who helped with the visit to the crypt of St Hilaire ('Theodore and his sister would light up for us with a candle the tomb of Sigebert's little daughter' (K166, P162)), later becomes the infamous maid of the baronne Putbus, the girl whose imminent arrival in Venice throws Marcel into a frenzy of erotically inspired inertia, threatening his mother's love ...

In its discrete but complex blending of motifs linking Combray and Venice, death and desire, memory and intuition, conscious artistry and chance association, the cathedral and the book, the Baptistery passage performs a resurrection of inner life through artistic intuition (like the passage describing the Martinville steeples, and unlike the madeleine and the paving-stone experiences).

But still the experience is not complete, still the narrator fails to interpret the pattern. It is only when he resurrects this primal Venetian scene by the accident of tripping over the paving stone which recalls the mosaic pavement of St Mark's that the revelation will be codified. Nonetheless, the Baptistery scene captures a complex psychological relationship with the world in a formal, artistic patterning as of a mosaic.

The figure of the mosaic itself is the major formal model of the *mise en abîme* and resurrection – the missing piece of the puzzle of Marcel's experience is found overlapping the pattern in the carpet; the paving stones of St Hilaire, St Mark's and the Guermantes' reecho vertiginously; the floor and walls of St Mark's are themselves one vast mosaic constructing a resurrectional message, as among the Baptistery mosaics there is the sudden reconstitution in artistically kaleidoscoped stone of the fragments of Marcel's intuitions of his mother, of his love and of his past, rebuilt into the jigsaw of memory, the mosaic of literature.[24]

Ruskin had announced the enormous importance of the artistic and religious creativity of the mosaics of St Mark's. He dismissed missal-painting as ornamentation, modern book-illustration as crude, sculpture as merging into architecture, stained-glass windows as hermetic, frescoes as feebly coloured:

Effective religious art, therefore, has always lain, and I believe must always lie, between the two extremes – of barbarous idol-fashioning on one side, and magnificent craftsmanship on the other [...] But of all these branches the most important are the inlaying and mosaic of the twelfth and thirteenth centuries, represented in a central manner by these mosaics of St Mark's [...] But the great mosaics of the twelfth and thirteenth centuries covered the walls and roofs of the churches with inevitable lustre; they could not be ignored or escaped from; their size rendered them majestic, their distance mysterious, their colour attractive. They did not pass into confused or inferior decorations; neither were they adorned with any evidences of skill or science, such as might withdraw the attention from their subjects. They were before the eyes of the devotee at every interval of his worship; vast shadowings forth of scenes to whose realization he looked forward, or of spirits whose presence he invoked'.

(The Stones of Venice, vol. II, ch. V, XXX).

But the reason for Marcel's partial failure in his quest at this stage of the work is probably the same as the reason for its qualified success – the Ruskinian inspiration. The artistic seriousness of Marcel takes him nearly to the truth. The idolatrous dependency on Ruskinian scholarship keeps him temporarily close to the level of Swann in his study of Vermeer,[25] still somewhat of a parasite, still unable to transpose his creative intuitions into writing. Yet there is hope. Previous experiences suggested by the pond at Montjouvain and the trees at Hudimesnil failed to reach articulation; the madeleine cake and the steeples produce a clear memory or a clear text, but their pleasure is inexplicable, their process obscure. In the Baptistery at last the act of memory is assimilated to the practice of artistic transposition. This is why it is this moment rather than any other which has to be resuscitated at the Guermantes'.

The reference to the act of writing and to the need to recreate emotion in art is carefully indicated by Proust, although Marcel does not self-consciously foreground it. At Marcel's hotel, the very blinds which filter the heat and light through the open windows shimmer like so much Biblical vellum ('thanks to the vellum which stirred outside the ever-open windows' (K III 661, P III 645)). The gospel is not just its holy message, it is the sacred book itself, the book as sacred human creation, complete with leather binding and gold tooling. This helps to alert us to the importance of the passage in connection with Marcel's literary vocation (he has recently been surprised and stimulated by the publication of his almost forgotten article – on the Martinville steeples – by the *Figaro* (K III 578–84,

P III 567–71)). The literary overtones are multiple, with the parch-
ment-like air and the book-like cathedral, and the major symbolism
of St Mark as the writer of the book is underscored by the fact
that Marcel visits St Mark's in order to write: about Ruskin, and,
as if thereby he had rubbed Aladin's lamp or relit the magic lantern
of his childhood, Combray returns again, both by the reminder of
being in his room in Combray at the same time of day, and by
the sensory reminiscence of the experience of shuttered coolness
allowing a savouring of the sunshine beyond:

at that hour when at Combray it was so pleasant to feel the sun close
at hand in the darkness preserved by the closed shutters, here, from top
to bottom of the marble staircase where one could no more tell than in
a Renaissance picture whether it was in a palace or on a galley, the same
coolness and the same sense of the splendour of the scene outside were
imparted.   (K III 660, P III 645).

Everywhere in the flamboyant, self-conscious city of Venice, one
is confronted by the narcissistic symbolism of the city and its self-
induced meanings. Everywhere St Mark's lion holds out his book,
with its confident message: 'Pax Tibi Marce Evangelista Meus.' By
some lapse of concentration Carpaccio himself, painter of the most
famous literary lion of all, to be found in the Ducal Palace, wrote
'AEvangelista' before correcting it to read 'Evangelista'. The resul-
tant text, with the altered initial 'E' of 'Evangelista' being the last
word of the left-hand page, looks surprisingly like 'PAX TIBI
MARCEL'. And even without this amusing accident we would find
it difficult not to note the obvious echo binding the two writers
Marc and Marcel.[26]
  The theme of salvation through writing has already been broached
at the beginning of *La prisonnière*. Bergotte, the famous novelist,
dies feeling that a tiny patch of yellow wall in Vermeer's *View of
Delft* is better than all his books:

At last he came to the Vermeer which he remembered as more striking,
more different from anything else he knew, but in which, thanks to the
critic's article, he noticed for the first time some small figures in blue, that
the sand was pink, and, finally, the precious substance of the tiny patch
of yellow wall. His dizziness increased; he fixed his gaze, like a child upon

13   Vermeer. *View of Delft*, Mauritshuis, The Hague.

a yellow butterfly that it wants to catch, on the precious little patch of wall. "That's how I ought to have written," he said. "My last books are too dry, I ought to have gone over them with a few layers of colour, made my language precious in itself, like this little patch of yellow wall."[27]

(K III 185, P III 187).

And he promptly dies, feeling that all his writing is useless compared to the layered texture of that patch of colour in a painting by Vermeer (the artist so long yet so fruitlessly studied by Swann). The patch, enclosed within the rest of the painting, is a miniature work in its own right, 'like some priceless specimen of Chinese art, of a beauty which was sufficient in itself'. He feels that real experience itself is more powerful and true than much art, and cites Venice as the type of that experience, overrunning the ability of an exhibition of Dutch painting to frame it:[28]

He walked past several pictures and was struck by the aridity and pointless-
ness of such an artifical kind of art, which was greatly inferior to the sunshine
of a windswept Venetian palazzo, or of an ordinary house by the sea.

(K III 185, P III 187).

Yet his own pessimism is questioned by the narrator: 'He was dead. Dead forever? Who can say?' For Bergotte has perhaps created his own formal intuitions, equivalent to Vermeer's protective lacquer of *mise en abîme*, without being conscious of it. And the narrator creates his own image of resurrection through the book; the butterfly lives, caught in his case:

They buried him, but all through that night of mourning, in the lighted
shop-windows, his books, arranged three by three, kept vigil like angels
with outspread wings and seemed, for him who was no more, the symbol
of his resurrection.   (K III 186, P III 188).

For Bergotte was not showing us that writing or painting is less valuable or lasting or true than the reality of the self or the city, whether Bergotte or Marcel, Venice or Delft. His comment meant that art must not imitate the appearance of reality, but reenact, re-create its sensory impact and texture through its own structure ('I ought to have gone over them with several layers of colour, made my language precious in itself, like this little patch of yellow wall'). It is this sensory reality which Marcel is recording unwittingly through his *Recherche*, although Proust often indicates the secret of his restructuring to us before he officially explains it in *Le temps retrouvé*. The sensory reality of Venice is not a diametrical alternative to art. It is a sensory reality which has to be transposed into a richly textured art which will preserve the emotional, subjective nature of Marcel's experience.

For Venice's bookish lion is not just the lion of St Mark, it is also, famously, the lion of St Jerome, translator of the Bible. On the same page that Marcel describes the struggles of his memory, figured as Albertine, to escape from its prison when stimulated by an accidental linguistic overlap between a sentence in his stock-broker's letter and a phrase spoken by Albertine's bathing assistant,

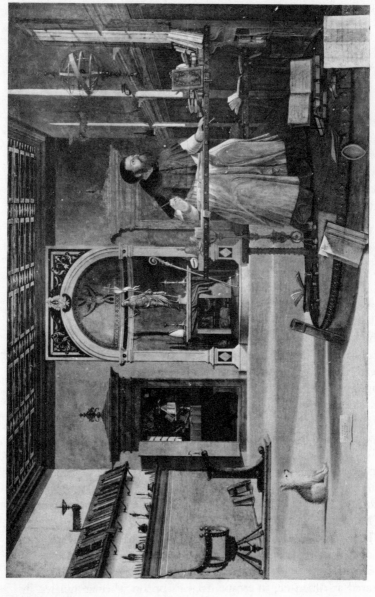

14 Vittore Carpaccio. *St Augustine in his studio*, Scuola Dalmata Dei SS. Giorgio e Trifone, Venice.

Marcel goes on to mention a second mini-resurrection, when the figure of an eagle at San Giorgio degli Schiavoni revived the memory of Albertine's ambiguous eagle rings. Carpaccio's paintings at San Giorgio, in addition to the admirable St George sequence of three paintings, include three paintings of Saint Jerome.[29] The last painting of this trio, the nearest painting to the door of the Scuola, shows not Jerome, but St Augustine. Jerome is gone: dead and martyred. But St Augustine in a famous vision sees him. St Augustine looks out through the church door to the city of Venice, to the present. Jerome will live on for ever in his translation. And in Carpaccio's painting, three by three, copies of the book that imply his salvation arise, with pages like angels' wings. Proust did, after all, say that literary creation was a kind of translation.

Few men can have ensured their immortality with a translation as effectively as St Jerome. We might wonder whether Proust, despite the enormous work of *A la recherche du temps perdu*, could still feel that his own survival might depend on his imperfect attempt to translate his inner truth through the medium of his translation of Ruskin. In *St Mark's Rest* the St Augustine painting – wrongly construed as an image of Jerome himself – is held by Ruskin's pupil Anderson to symbolise resurrection through the Book, with a capital R:

The two great volumes leaning against the wall by the arm-chair are the same thing, the closed testaments. There is a very prominent illuminated R on one of the documents under the table (I think you have written of it as Greek in its lines): I cannot but fancy it is the initial letter of 'Resurrectio'.

(*St Mark's Rest*, p. 26).

But to return to Proust's own moment of apotheosis. The scholar will find it particularly satisfying to know that in the Baptistery, with its beautiful thirteenth-century mosaics, is the tomb of the Doge Dandolo, who was responsible for the decoration of the Baptistery. He is entombed in stone within his stone creation. Ruskin takes up the story in one of his most beautiful prose passages:

We are in a low vaulted room; vaulted, not with arches, but with small cupolas starred with gold, and chequered with gloomy figures: in the centre is a bronze font charged with rich bas reliefs, a small figure of the Baptist standing above it in a single ray of light that glances across the narrow room, dying as it falls from a window high in the wall, and the first thing

15   Tomb of Doge Dandolo, St Mark's, Venice (Photo P. Collier).

that it strikes, and the only thing that it strikes brightly, is a tomb. We hardly know if it be a tomb indeed; for it is like a narrow couch set beside the window, low-roofed and curtained, so that it might seem, but that it is some height above the pavement, to have been drawn towards the window, that the sleeper might be awakened early; – only there are two angels who have drawn the curtain back, and are looking down upon him. Let us look also, and thank that gentle light that rests upon his forehead for ever, and dies away upon his breast.

The face is of a man, in middle life, but there are two deep furrows right across the forehead, dividing it like the foundations of a tower [...] The rest of the features are singularly small and delicate, the lips sharp, perhaps the sharpness of death being added to that of the natural lines; but there is a sweet smile upon them, and a deep serenity upon the whole countenance.   (*The Stones of Venice*, Tr. Ed., pp. 105–6).

Proust's sleeper at the centre of a whole world, Marcel dreaming at the centre of the mosaic of his *Recherche*, the writer eternally living on in his work, is resuscitated by each new reader, who raises the stone effigy from its sculpted tomb.

Ruskin portrays the death of St Jerome, as painted at San Giorgio by Carpaccio, in terms similar to those used for the Doge Dandolo – the body again becoming part of an inlaid marble pattern, and its very petrification indicating through its unearthly stillness the potential of resurrection:

> But St Jerome himself in the midst of them, the eager heart of him quiet, to such uttermost quietness, – the body lying – look – absolutely flat like clay, as if it had been beat down, and clung, clogged, all along to the marble. Earth to earth indeed. Level clay and inlaid rock now all one – and the noble head senseless as a stone, with a stone for its pillow.
>
> (*St Mark's Rest*, pp. 21–2).

And perhaps the topos of artistic pacification and petrification of passion was prepared in the beautiful passage where Marcel contemplates the sleeping figure of Albertine in *La Prisonnière*:

> It was indeed a dead woman that I saw when, presently, I entered her room. She had fallen asleep as soon as she lay down; her sheets, wrapped round her body like a shroud, had assumed, with their elegant folds, the rigidity of stone. It was as though, reminiscent of certain mediaeval Last Judgments, the head alone was emerging from the tomb, awaiting in its sleep the Archangel's trumpet. [...] And so I remained, in the fur-lined coat which I had not taken off since my return from the Verdurins', beside that twisted body, that allegorical figure. Allegorising what? My death? My work?[30] (K III 366–7, P III 359–60).

Once again the last judgement is an *aesthetic* judgement, and the morphic, oneiric vision transforms chaotic passion and suffering into a still, artistic sense.

Ruskin's description of the eternally sleeping artist is no doubt inspired by the opening lines of Dante's *Inferno*:

> Nel mezzo del cammin di nostra vita
> mi ritrovai per una selva oscura
> che la diritta via era smarrita.
> Ah quanto a dir qual era è cosa dura
> esta selva selvaggia e aspra e forte
> che nel pensier rinova la paura!
> Tant' è amarra che poco è piu morte;
> ma per trattar del ben ch'io vi trovai,
> dirò dell'altre cose ch'i v'ho scorte.
> Io non so ben ridir com' io v'entrai,
> tant'era pieno di sonno a quel punto
> che la verace via abbandonai.   (*Inferno*, I).

In the middle of the journey of our life I came to myself within a dark wood where the straight way was lost. Ah, how hard a thing it is to tell of that wood, savage and harsh and dense, the thought of which renews my fear! So bitter is it that death is hardly more. But to give account of the good which I found there I will tell of the other things I noted there. I cannot rightly tell how I entered there, I was so full of sleep at that moment when I left the true way. (tr. J. D. Sinclair).

But this whole picture of the artist caught at the turning point of his life in confusion and darkness, with the effort of narrative recall being likened to death, and yet the trajectory of salvation to be retraced requiring the narration of the erratic path which led there, is even closer to the enterprise of Proust's hero. Marcel's whole search is a confusing plunge into the night of the soul, from a position of median wandering, in order to discover the creative darkness which both blinded him as man and yet provides the material for his art. Marcel's two ways, that of Guermantes and that of Méséglise, are a mental projection of a man 'in middle life', and in a sense are like 'two deep furrows right across the forehead, dividing it like the foundations of a tower'. The opening dream of Combray (cf. above, p. 119–20), was perhaps a Dantesque dream, as well as an Ursuline one:

> Quale è colui che suo dannaggio sogna,
>   che sognando desidera sognare,
>   sì quel ch'è, come non fosse, agogna
> tal mi fec'io, non possendo parlare,
>   che disïava scusarmi, e scusava
>   me tuttavia, e nol mi credea fare. (*Inferno*, XXX).

Like one that dreams of harm to himself and, dreaming, wishes it a dream, so that he longs for that which is as if it were not, I became such that, unable to speak, I wished to excuse myself and did excuse myself all the while, not thinking that I did. (tr. J. D. Sinclair).

And the dream thought of inarticulacy, seen as a gesture of moral eloquence, and expressed paradoxically with the most sophisticated rhetorical flourish, is repeated powerfully in Venice, as we have seen in Chapter 5 (pp. 66–70) where it is projected in the guise of one of Giotto's vices, Envy. And at the heart of the Baptistery passage itself we have the Dantesque (or Giottesque) *mise en abîme*, as Marcel and his mother enter the Baptisery and encroach on its plastic forms: 'treading underfoot the marble and glass mosaics of the paving, in front of us the wide arcades whose curved pink surfaces have been slightly warped by time' (K III 660–1, P III 646), pressing into the mosaic which has already been inflected by time, only to find that in the enfolding present of the narrative, this very act of moral enshrining of an aesthetic intuition, has been interiorised as part of the overarching mosaic of memory preserved in the crystalline structuring of art:

A time has now come when, remembering the baptistery of St Mark's – contemplating the waters of the Jordan in which St John immerses Christ, while the gondola awaited us at the landing-stage of the Piazzetta – it is no longer a matter of indifference to me that, beside me in that cool penumbra, there should have been a woman draped in her mourning with the respectful and enthusiastic fervour of the old woman in Carpaccio's *St Ursula* in the Accademia, and that that woman, with her red cheeks and sad eyes and in her black veils, whom nothing can ever remove from that softly lit sanctuary of St Mark's where I am always sure to find her because she has her place reserved there as immutably as a mosaic, should be my mother.

(K III 661, P III 646).

The mother is inserted inside the work of art woven by the consciousness of the artist, but it is her presence in his memory that inserts his consciousness inside the aesthetically powerful mosaic of the Basilica. In very similar fashion Beatrice holds Dante in her transcendental power throughout the *Commedia*, whilst thereby enabling him to struggle through the confusion of his experience to the point where his art will (and already does, like Proust's) preserve her, in her turn, in the transcendental form of his writing.[31]

Conclusion

'Ne vous plaignez pas de ne pas avoir appris. *Il n'y a rien à savoir*'. Marcel Proust to Marie Nordlinger

A la recherche du temps perdu starts and finishes with a spectacular overlap of experience, where an event embedded within another event suddenly burgeons, engulfing the event which originally contained it. In the opening section of *Combray*, the middle-aged narrator meditates on the difficulty of situating himself temporally and spatially when he awakes, and the difficulty of stabilising any visions of the past which do happen to materialise, but then recounts a moment of seemingly magical power. While drinking limeflower tea with his mother, and tasting a madeleine-cake dipped in the tea, he suddenly finds himself as if transported physically into the time and place where he had once previously experienced the same taste: in childhood, in Combray.

This process of 'involuntary' memory is partly one of sensory association. A present sensory experience brings back a similar one from the past, but the past sensory experience returns enveloped in its content – physical, intellectual, emotional. The past moment is resurrected as fresh as when it happened, or fresher, because it is undimmed by deliberate reflection. Thus past experience resurrects a past self which had seemed dead and gone.

Yet the madeleine incident is even more striking for its layered structuring of experience, memory and sensation. The experience was first encoded, protected, embedded in sensory form – teatime at Combray was resumed within the taste of a madeleine-cake, which had been only a fragment of the whole teatime experience. Then, that sensory experience – the taste – is stored within mind and body, buried and yet simultaneously preserved by layers of later experience, whose associations will release it when they are triggered by a suitable stimulus.

This embedding is exemplified in the cake. It is at first a small part of its context, immersed in the tea then engulfed by the mouth, it is only a minute fragment of the whole situation of Combray. It has the form of a 'scallop shell' (K 1 48, P 1 45). But, just as the sea shell houses a live creature within its compact bounds, so the porous madeleine cake internalises the taste and smell of the tea, as well as all the sensory, emotional and intellectual experience associated with the moment of consumption. From being a fragmentary part of the wider context which contains it, it comes to contain, by a process of synechdoche, a concentrated model of the whole. This whole matrix of experience is protected from deterioration by its non-intellectual but nonetheless formally organised configuration – our past remains hidden in the opaque, sensory code of such an object:

And so it is with our own past. It is a labour in vain to attempt to recapture it: all the efforts of our intellect must prove futile. The past is hidden somewhere outside the realm, beyond the reach of intellect, in some material object (in the sensation which that material object will give us) of which we have no inkling. (K 1 47–8, P 1 44).

When the older narrator comes to eat a similar cake, he unlocks a part of his former sensory self. He places the cake within his mouth. But the 'content' permeates his senses, and comes to enclose him within the experience of his past. The past self is at first an internal image, contained within him, yet gradually it invades and suffuses him:

An exquisite pleasure had invaded my senses [...] filling me with a precious essence; or rather this essence was not in me, it *was* me. [...]
Undoubtedly what is thus palpitating in the depths of my being must be the image, the visual memory which, being linked to that taste, is trying to follow it into my conscious mind. (K 1 48–9, P 1 46).

The self which believed that it contained the cake, is engulfed by the overflowing presence of the cake. The present self shrinks, and is enclosed within the more powerful presence of the past self.

The past self then releases its experience of the previous cake, and the past experience associated with it. Thus the village and the child, contained within the cake, flower within the narrator's present self, then take him over, until he again becomes an infant inhabitant of Combray, which now resumes its encirclement of his world:

and as in the game wherein the Japanese amuse themselves by filling a porcelain bowl with water and steeping in it little pieces of paper which until then are without character or form, but, the moment they become wet, stretch and twist and take on colour and distinctive shape, become flowers or houses or people, solid and recognizable, so in that moment all the flowers in our garden and in M. Swann's park, and the water-lilies on the Vivonne and the good folk of the village and their little dwellings and the parish church and the whole of Combray and its surroundings, taking shape and solidity, sprang into being, town and gardens alike, from my cup of tea.   (K I 51, P I 47–8).

The seeds linking this *mise en abîme* with Venice must have been sown very early in Proust's mind by Marie Nordlinger. She recalls that it was she who in 1904 sent Proust some tiny Japanese toys, which were to become the model for the *mise en abîme* of memory:

One day I had succeeded in sending him something he had never seen before: little Japanese paper pellets, flowers, figurines or houses, which open out when placed in water.

and that Proust replied with typical hyperbole:

Thank you for your marvellous, secret flowers, which allowed me this evening to "recreate Spring", as Madame de Sévigné says, but an innocent, freshwater Spring. Thanks to you, the electric light of my dark bedroom flowered into a Far-Eastern Spring.   (*Lettres à une amie*, p. x; p. 45).

And in an otherwise forgettable poem to Marie, Proust verbally encases her gift of a translucent pink enamel (which had already set the hawthorn he loved in an aquatic, coloured, vitreous setting which looks forward to Marcel's church window, or the Balbec seaside), so that he inserts her embedded flower within his own formal verse, thus transforming her romantic, natural image into a gothic Venetian marine:

> L'émail marin qu'enclôt le frêle cuivre d'or,
> Sur les flots interdits fait palpiter ta rame.

La matière est fermée: entr'ouvre-la Sésame ...
A tes goûts préférés je veux joindre les miens ...
Tu sauras retrouver les vitraux dans tes jeux.
(Lettres à une amie, pp. 36–7, & cf. p. 118)

Enamel seas enclosed in fragile gilded bronze
Push your pulsating oar across the inhibited waves.
Ease open, Sesame, the secret locked within ...
To your most favoured tastes I want to marry mine ...
Allow my stained-glass panes to infiltrate your game.

Marie's gold frame already provided the artistic frame of the enamel with a further layer of protection and self-reflexive artistry: Proust's insertion of her image into the framework of a stained-glass window provides a second-degree twist of artistry: the golden frame, which could figure a painting, becomes miniaturised, becomes only the leaden border of a fragment of stained-glass, contained within a wider window, which in its turn is only part of the larger artefact of Venice. The waters of Venice enclose the hawthorn, only to be transmuted into Venetian glass and enclosed by Proust's alexandrines. And, simultaneously, the layering and embedding protects the ambiguity of passion circulating throughout this exchange of natural, artistic and verbal gifts: the traditionally romantic image of the gondola evoked by Proust is destabilised by the covertly but disturbingly erotic 'interdits' (inhibited), 'palpiter' (pulsating) and 'entr'ouvre' (ease open). Desire is reechoed as it were in inner courtyards, perceived through the framing doorways of Proust's *mise en abîme*.

The transformation which produces *La recherche*, however, is the one which reprocesses and splits the Japanese toys and the miniature enamel, and produces on the one hand the epiphany of the madeleine, with the great textual flowering which it entails, on the other hand the whole artistic structure of Venice. We have seen that the initial inspiration the toys afforded Proust was Venetian rather than domestic – he mentions safe springtime travel ('printemps [...] inoffensif'), which was his reason for visiting Venice rather than Florence (see p. 12 above); eventually the river Vivonne will emerge from his 'fluviatile' (freshwater), but the canals of Venice are already potentially there, while the limeflower tea is not yet. The oriental associations of Venice are evoked in the 'Far-Eastern', its erotic and romantic aspects in its 'inhibited waves' and 'singular oar', the *Arabian Nights* in 'ease open, Sesame'. This is the world of the asthmatic but excitable young traveller, rather than that of the dull, tea-drinking narrator. Moreover, the imagery also evokes the photographic darkroom with its development of full-flowering prints from dried paper negatives, suggesting how powerfully in Proust's mind the phenomenon of the rebirth of the lost self was linked to the Venetian experience.

As Proust's letter and poem already show him inserting the spring hawthorn blossom and stained-glass windows of Combray and the river Vivonne inside the larger models of the golden picture-frames, gondolas and equivocal desires of Venice, so the text of *A la recherche du temps perdu* uses a similar system of *mise en abîme* to alert us to the way in which the childhood experience of Combray will be stored and later released through a Venetian process. The town that springs up from within the teacup, like the paper models that are revived by being plunged into a bowl of water, is a prolepsis, first of the dream of Venice, where the gothic city arises from the middle of the sea (see above p. 68), and, second, of the internal redoubling of the structure of Venice itself when Marcel visits it, its squares expanding within the logically smaller frames of its *rios* and *calli*. It is also an advance model of the whole resurrection of the self through the medium of artistry in the Baptistery, as the shrivelled, cramped figures of Marcel, his mother and Albertine expand in the context of the liquid city, crystallising into a concentrated artistic structuring, which will await its second liquid baptism.

As Combray flowers accidentally in the teacup, so when the Venetian experience looms at the end of *La prisonnière*, it is in terms of a garden flowering in water, evoked through the blue and gold of a Fortuny dress, which had been intended to foster a different desire:

But all of a sudden the scene changed; it was the memory, no longer of old impressions but of an old desire, only recently reawakened by the Fortuny gown in blue and gold, that spread before me another spring, a spring not leafy at all but on the contrary suddenly stripped of its trees and flowers by the name that I had just murmured to myself: "Venice"; a decanted springtime, which is reduced to its essence [...] of a blue and virginal water, springlike without bud or blossom [...] that fabulous garden of fruits and birds in coloured stone, flowering in the midst of the sea which kept it refreshed. (K III 419–20, P III 412).

In its turn, Venice had become compressed and codified, until it is finally revived through Marcel's experience of tripping on a paving stone, triggering a reaction similar to that he felt when walking on the uneven flagstones of the Baptistery of St Mark's, resurrecting the past self who had had that Venetian experience, and expanding the 'dried', miniature image of memory

[...] at the moment when the unevenness of the two paving-stones had extended in every direction and dimension the dessicated and insubstantial images which I normally had of Venice and St Mark's and of all the sensations which I had felt there, reuniting the piazza to the cathedral, the landing stage to the piazza, the canal to the landing stage, and to all that the eyes see the world of desires which is seen only by the mind [...].

(K III 909–10, P III 876).

Memories of Balbec, at first frozen in the folds of a napkin recalling the overlapping waves, swell to suggest Fortuny's fabric and St Mark's architecture, in a new mnemonic structure engulfing the rememberer:

The marine dining-room of Balbec, with its damask linen prepared like so many altar-cloths to receive the setting sun, had sought to shatter the solidity of the Guermantes mansion, to force open its doors.

(K III 908, P III 874).

But as these memories displace experience like great waves, they in their turn are invaded, infiltrated by the all-embracing past:

I had remained in a state of ecstasy on the uneven paving-stones or before the cup of tea, endeavouring to prolong or to reproduce the momentary appearances of the Combray or the Balbec or the Venice which invaded only to be driven back, which rose up only at once to abandon me in the midst of the new scene which somehow, nevertheless, the past had been able to permeate. (K III 908, P III 875).

He speaks of 'the being three times, four times brought back to life within me' as if it were a miniature embedded person (K III 908, P III 875), but, ultimately, all these sensations are the creation of that self within the self, that small, lost, past person who nonetheless encloses a world:

so complete are these resurrections of the past during the second that they last, that they [...] oblige [...] our will to choose between the various projects which those distant places suggest to us, they force our whole self to believe that it is surrounded by these places or at least to waver doubtfully between them and the places where we are now.   (K III 908, P III 875).

The process is one of transference and invasion, whereby Combray becomes miniaturised and contained within one of its characters, whose teacup then releases Combray until it floats around him. But the spiral structure of memory and experience is ultimately completed by a concomitant spiralling of art, whereby Venice is enclosed within Fortuny dresses and Carpaccio paintings, then stored in a sensory experience of its stones until released from them again to engulf Marcel. Proust operates a complex mechanism, whereby the experience of surrounding, containing space becomes internalised, contained within the subject, and the subject himself becomes projectible and expressible in terms of an experience first absorbed environmentally, then reformulated in terms of a new, artistic or textual structure.

The catalyst for this transformation is that of involuntary, sensory memory, whose structural layering and repetition of experience is a basic form of artistic creativity. The premiss appears to be that each node of experience is stored, protected and structured by its sensory and imaginative context, described metaphorically as colour-coded, interlocking but watertight stone or glass jars – an extraordinary image yielding a vision of the whole self as a vast honeycomb of a mosaic:

I noticed cursorily that the differences which exist between every one of our real impressions – differences which explain why a uniform depiction of life cannot bear much resemblance to the reality – derive probably from the following cause: the slightest word that we have said, the most insignificant action that we have performed at any one epoch of our life was surrounded by, and coloured by the reflection of, things which logically had no connexion with it and which later have been separated from it by our intellect which could make nothing of them for its own rational purposes, things, however, in the midst of which – here the pink reflection of the evening upon the flower-covered wall of a country restaurant, a feeling of hunger, the desire for women, the pleasure of luxury; there the blue volutes of the morning sea and, enveloped in them, phrases of music half emerging like the shoulders of water-nymphs – the simplest act or gesture remains immured as within a thousand sealed vessels, each one of them filled with things of a colour, a scent, a temperature that are absolutely different one from another, vessels moreover, which being disposed over the whole range of our years, during which we have never ceased to change if only in our dreams and our thoughts, are situated at the most various moral altitudes and give us the sensation of extraordinarily diverse atmospheres. (K III 902–3, P III 870).

The repetition and restructuring into art of even such a simple moment of experience – with its diffuse sensations of lingering warmth, fading light, flowers at sunset perceived against a wall at Rivebelle – require transposition into a different material from that required for a morning in Venice:

And I observed in passing that for the work of art which I now, though I had not yet reached a conscious resolution, felt myself ready to undertake, this distinctness of different events would entail very considerable difficulties. For I should have to execute the successive parts of my work in a succession of different materials; what would be suitable for mornings beside the sea or afternoons in Venice would be quite wrong if I wanted to depict those evenings at Rivebelle when, in the dining-room that opened on to the garden, the heat began to resolve into fragments and sink back into the ground, while a sunset glimmer still illuminated the roses on the walls of the restaurant and the last water-colours of the day were still visible in the sky – this would be a new and distinct material, of a transparency and a sonority that were special, compact, cold after warmth, rose-pink. (K III 904, P III 870–1).

Here the clear, cool, compact, coloured material sounds very like the glass of the mosaic. And the key to recreating a whole self, through a process of artistic transposition, implies the search for the linguistic equivalent of the aesthetic restructuring of fragments operated by the mosaic.

Genette has likened this process of transposition and reversal to the rhetorical transfer of qualities operated in metaphor, calling it a 'typically baroque artifice whereby substances in contact exchange their predicates to enter into this relationship of the "reciprocal meta-phor"' (*Figures* III, p. 54). Proust's idea of style is based on rejecting serial description, and regrouping units of the description into struc-tured compositions; the artist

can describe a scene by describing one after another the innumerable objects which at a given moment were present at a particular place, but truth will be attained by him only when he takes two different objects, states the connexion between them – a connexion analagous in the world of art to the unique connexion which in the world of science is provided by the law of causality – and encloses them in the necessary links of a well-wrought style; truth, and life too – can be attained by us only when, by comparing a quality common to two sensations, we succeed in extracting their common essence and in reuniting them to each other, liberated from the contingencies of time, within a metaphor.

(K III 924–5, P III 889).

The relationship of metaphor to mosaic is perhaps finally made plain by the process of embedding exemplified in one of the above quotations. In the very act of theorising the process of transpos-ition, Proust embeds his diction in concentric syntactic circles. The phrase: 'And I observed in passing that [...] this distinctness of different events would entail very considerable difficulties' embeds within itself an internalised clause vastly expanding the central 'that': 'for the work of art which I now [...] felt myself ready to undertake', which clause embeds a further, internalised qualifying clause at its heart, opening an abyss beneath the conscious surface of the sentence, almost as if the buried clause were its 'unconscious': 'though I had not yet reached a conscious resolution'. And while formulating an aesthetic and performing it syntactically, the text operates a parallel process of connotation, turning the 'pink reflection of the evening' into 'the last water-colours of the day', transposing the natural into the artistic through metaphor. We have seen how the paving-stones of the Baptistery restructure through *mise en abîme* the experience which had already settled into a mosaic structure protecting contingent desire and perception. This process of fragmenting, compressing, layering, followed by a spiralling regrouping, becomes the phrase structure of Proust's

Recherche. Proust argued that writing was a kind of translation. In construing the narrative structure of his prose, as much as its sense, we reconstruct a world. Reading Proust is a process of re-creation.

Notes

1. Proust's travels: 'Impossible venir: mensonge suit'

1 Which it was, finally, in 1912.

2 *Corr.* II, pp. 384–7 & 396–7.

3 *Corr.* II. p. 396: 'If you were to go to Venice let me know for it is *possible* [...] that I might go! Alas, my hay fever makes Florence imposs-ible for me' (letter to Marie Nordlinger, 25 or 26 April 1900).

4 *Corr.* II, p. 399: 'Marcel very oppressed, unable to breathe or sleep but *less* ill than he was in Venice' (letter from Reynaldo Hahn to a friend, soon after 21 June 1900).

5 *Corr.* III, p. 199 contains the sublime telegram from Antoine Bibesco to Marcel Proust: 'Reçu lettres aujourdh'hui navré Asti i à 10 heures ecrirai una deco toi. – Antoine', which was, however, a weak excuse around 21–24 December for not rearranging the projected meeting for 1 January. *Corr.* III, p. 204 shows Proust trying to find an excuse in his brother's forthcoming marriage to avoid meeting Antoine in Egypt or Romania, and by the very elaborateness of his protestations of readi-ness to go to Strehaïa or Ragusa in February or March, despite fiendish complications, makes it clear he will never quite make it (letter to Antoine Bibesco 27 Dec. 1902). This culminates in a piece of hysterical textual exegesis by Proust of a letter from Bibesco inviting him to Constanti-nople where Proust's objection turns on the interpretation of a word in Bibesco's letter as 'dès' rather than 'ou' (*Corr.* III, pp. 212–15, letter to Antoine Bibesco 19 Jan 1903; *Corr.* III, pp. 223–4, letter to Antoine Bibesco 26 Jan 1903).

6 Cf. *Corr.* II, p. 412 re his second visit in October 1900. The only trace of his second trip is his signature in the visitors' book in the Armenian monastery on the island of San Lazzaro on 19 October 1900 (cf. Painter, I, 294).

7 *Corr.* III, p. 155–63, esp. p. 160: 'Ruskin has intoxicated me. All this profane painting makes me ... [me fait ...]' (note to Leon Yeatman from Dordrecht, 11, 12 or 13 October 1902).

8 Marie Nordlinger's account: 'On a radiant May morning, my aunt, Reynaldo and I did in fact see Marcel and his mother arrive in Venice. A few hours later, in the shadow of St Mark's, we started to correct our translation of the *Bible of Amiens*. I remember once, in a moment of dark, stormy weather, that Marcel and I took refuge inside the basilica, and there, together, we read passages from *The Stones of Venice* of a beauty worthy of our surroundings' (Nordlinger, p. IX). Of a page of *St Mark's Rest* Proust says:

> For me, this page has not only the charm of having been read in the baptistry of Saint Mark's, in those blessed days when, with some other disciples "in spirit and in truth" of the master, we would go about Venice in a gondola, listening to his teachings by the water's edge, and landing at each one of the temples that seemed to spring up from the sea to offer us the object of his descriptions and the very image of his thought, to give life to his books, whose immortal reflection shines on them today. (*ORR* 82, *CSB* P 738).

He confirms Marie Nordlinger's account:

> I remember having read it for the first time in St Mark's itself, during a dark and tempestuous hour, when the mosaics shone only by their own physical light and with an internal, an earthly gold to which the Venetian sun, which sets even the angels of the campaniles ablaze, mingled nothing of its own; the emotion I felt, as I was reading this page, among all those angels which shone forth from the surrounding darkness, was great, and yet perhaps not very pure. (*Post Scriptum à la Bible d'Amiens*, *ORR* 53, *CSB* P 133)

9 *Corr.* II. p. 387, 7 or 8 February to Marie Nordlinger: 'If ever you were to send me other extracts from letters or passages from Ruskin what interests me of his above all at the moment is what he wrote on the French cathedrals, except the one at Amiens [...] All my labours are finished but if in ten years time you come across a line of his I shall still be as interested as I am today.' Even when he thanks Marie for pointing out to him Ruskin's *The Poetry of Architecture; Giotto and his Work in Padua* (*Corr.* II, p. 391, March 1900), he merely asks: 'does it contain any reference to the cathedrals?'.

10 *Corr.* III, p. 196 (to Antoine Bibesco, 20 Dec 1902): 'Nothing I do is real work, but only research, translation, etc. It is enough to awaken my ambition to achieve something myself, but not enough, naturally, to slake that thirst at all. Since after that long period of lethargy I turned

my thoughts inward for the first time, into my own mind, I have been feeling the whole void of my life. A hundred fictional characters, a thousand ideas have been asking me to give them bodily form like those shades in *The Odyssey* who ask Ulysses to let them drink a little blood to bring them back to life, and he has to sweep them aside with his sword. I have awakened the sleeping bee and I can feel his cruel sting much more strongly than his powerless wings. I had enslaved my intelligence to my leisure. In untying its fetters I thought merely to liberate a slave, but I have given myself a master, whom I do not have the physical strength to satisfy and who would kill me if I didn't resist him.' And, later, he rejects the idea of translating *St Mark's Rest*, 'for otherwise I would die without ever having written anything of my own' (Nordlinger p. 80); and he confirms the distinction between translating other people's visions and 'translating' his own: 'Are you working on something? I myself have stopped. I've put an end to the phase of translation, which was encouraged by Mama. And as for translating out of myself, I can't face up to it any more' (Nordlinger, p. 105, 8 Dec 1906).

11 Yet, in 1917, living in a Paris suffering from the strain of war, Proust apparently felt tempted to remove to Venice and live in a palazzo with his favourite string quartet! (Painter, II, 244).

12 Corr. II, p. 397 (to Leon Yeatman, shortly before 3 May 1900).

13 Jackson, p. 89–118.

14 *Corr*, III, p. 173, (to Antoine Bibesco, 10 November 1902): 'And I do not think that their power to appease will ever be disarmed', he says of Ruskin's words.

15 *Corr*. III, p. 448 (to Mme de Noailles, 3 December 1903): 'But now Mama has heard that I abandoned the Ruskin she has got it into her head that it would have been Papa's pride and joy, and that he had been looking forward impatiently to the publication day.' And so the dutiful son completed his work and dedicated *La Bible d'Amiens* to his father's memory:
    '*In Memory of My Father* Stricken while working on 24 November 1903. Died on 26 November this translation is dedicated with tender affection' (*ORR* 3, *CSB* P 722).

16 And he justifies this openly in his preface to *La Bible d'Amiens*: 'There is no better way of becoming aware of one's own feelings than to try to recreate in oneself what a master has felt' (*ORR* 60, *CSB* P 140). However, we can see that this justifies a kind of critical empathy, but does not suggest how it would help the creative artist.

17 Jean Autret, *L'influence de Ruskin sur la vie, les idées et l'œuvre de Marcel Proust*, Genève 1955.

18 Cf. *ORR* 128–9, *CSB* P 194. The preface (published by Proust as 'Jour-
nées de lecture') still accords pride of place to Dutch art (*ORR* 118–19,
CSB P 181–2). Proust had been more recently to Holland. But the
Sésame preface, rather than the 'Journées' version, ends in a veritable
Venetian apotheosis (*ORR* 128–9, *CSB* P, pp. 811–12).

2. Desire, ideal, remembrance – the Venetian syndrome

1 The whole conceit is perhaps surreptitiously motivated by the unmen-
tioned but obvious presence at St Mark's of the four great bronze horses.

2 Sometimes at dusk as I returned to the hotel I felt that the Albertine
of long ago, invisible to my eyes, was nevertheless enclosed within me
as in the *Piombi* of an inner Venice, the tight lid of which some incident
occasionally lifted to give me a glimpse of that past.

Thus for instance one evening a letter from my stockbroker reopened
for me for an instant the gates of the prison in which Albertine dwelt
within me, alive, but so remote, so profoundly buried that she remained
inaccessible to me [...] And these words which had never recurred to
my mind acted like an "Open sesame!" upon the hinges of the prison
door (K III 654–5, P III 641).

There is surely a reminiscence here by Proust of Nerval's *Sylvie*, where
the hero is likewise reading a stock-market report, and a note in the
paper referring to the annual archery festival in his home town sends
his mind racing back to the long-forgotten Sylvie, at the very moment
when the same paper reveals that he has won the financial means to
seek her out again. Although Proust has organised a different sequence
of events, the equation of desire with the stock market and with newspaper reading and the random memories this evokes, appears unmistak-
ably Nervalian.

3 Perhaps it is memory itself which is the true *Prisonnière* and *Fugitive*
in these volumes concerned with Albertine and Venice?

4 Proust's allusion is difficult to trace. There do not appear to be any
obvious eagles or figures of St John in Carpaccio's paintings in the
Scuola San Giorgio (although the Scuola does have historical associations with the Knights of St John). The evangelical eagle is omnipresent
in Venice, but one possible source of Proust's reference could well be
Carpaccio's *Presentation of Jesus in the Temple* (in the Accademia), which
was Ruskin's favourite painting, and where the presiding priest is portrayed as St John, and his cloak is covered with Johnian eagles (cf.
Whittick, *Ruskin's Venice*, p. 18, re. Ruskin's *Guide to the Principal Pictures
in the Academy of Fine Arts*).

5 Towards the end of *Du côté de chez Swann* the narrator recounts his first attempt to write, as a youth, trying to describe what he felt to be the secret essence of some distant steeples which appeared to be moving, and feeling a thrill of pleasure at self-expression, despite his intellectual frustration at failing to grasp their inner meaning (K I 196–9, P I 180–2).

6 In *Du côté de chez Swann* the mature but not yet enlightened narrator feels inexplicable bliss when the taste of a madeleine cake dipped in lime tea suddenly recalls occasions in his childhood at Combray when he experienced the same taste (K I 48–51, P I 44–8).

3. *Some Proustian pretexts: Titian, Racine, Vergil, Ruskin*

1 Marcel has already noted in Paris how his furtive contact with girls resembling Albertine, or connected with, or likely to have been desired by her, is as frustrating as trying to possess a painting:

> No doubt it is only in one's mind that one possesses things, and one does not possess a picture because it hangs in one's dining-room if one is incapable of understanding it, or a landscape because one lives in it without even looking at it [...] Andrée, and these other women, all of them in relation to Albertine – like Albertine herself in relation to Balbec – were to be numbered among those substitute pleasures, replacing one another in a gradual declension, which enable us to dispense with the pleasure to which we can no longer attain, a trip to Balbec or the love of Albertine, pleasures which (just as going to the Louvre to look at a Titian consoles us for not being able to go to Venice where it originally was), separated one from another by indistinguishable gradations, convert one's life into a series of concentric, contiguous, harmonic and graduated zones, encircling an initial desire which has set the tone, eliminated everything that does not combine with it, applied the dominant colour. (K III 563, P III 552).

The topos of the substitute Titian is thus carefully prepared in advance.

2 'Every person we love, indeed to a certain extent every person, is to us like Janus, presenting to us a face that pleases us if the person leaves us, a dreary face if we know him or her to be at our perpetual disposal. In the case of Albertine, the prospect of her continued society was painful to me' (K III 179, P III 181). Cf. also K III 471–4, P III 462–5, and my pp. 87–9.

3 The *Phèdre* quotation is no doubt, like the Titian reference, a deliberate recurrence of an earlier textual structure. The disappearance of Albertine

in *La Fugitive* coincides with the death of La Berma. This reminds Marcel of her Phèdre recitation, and his two conflicting visions of it are subsumed now into a third reading, echoing Marcel's own experience of love, that is, we believe we can live without someone until their possession by somebody else makes us suffer and realise the extent of our desire, or alternatively, we think we would welcome the loss of someone we do possess, but their departure makes us suffer. Marcel, then, interprets Phèdre in similar terms: she delays articulating her passion until the imminent departure of Hippolyte stings her into understanding her desire, but when he shows that he misinterprets her advances, she regrets her declaration, and feels a murderous jealousy of Aricie: Marcel feels that her jealous regrets are the same as his feelings about having written asking Albertine to return, and then instantly wishing he had not despatched the letter. Thus incestuous jealousy in Phèdre is already linked with the disappearance and possible reappearance of Albertine (K III 467–9, P III 460). Moreover, this concentrated exegesis of *Phèdre* was rapidly followed by Françoise's analysis of the treacherous eagle-rings – thus the rapid recurrence in Venice of a quotation from the same scene of *Phèdre* and an echo of the same eagle motif show that Marcel's experience is starting to repeat itself in significant patterns. The death of La Berma and Albertine and the jealous projection of Titian and structures from *Phèdre* in *La Fugitive* in their turn were figured in advance in *A l'ombre des jeunes filles en fleurs:*

> I should enjoy the same rapture as on the day when a gondola would deposit me at the foot of the Titian of the Frari or the Carpaccios of San Giorgio dei Schiavoni, were I ever to hear Berma recite the lines beginning,
>
> On dit qu'un prompt départ vous éloigne de nous,
> Seigneur . . .   (K I 475, P I 440–1).

4   In an earlier draft the mother's token mourning was more conventionally intended to keep up appearances: 'Mamma sat [. . .] waiting for me and reading the while, wearing the pretty straw hat that netted her face in a white veil and was intended to make her look "dressed" enough for meeting people in the restaurant or out walking' (*BWSB* 66, *CSB* F 122). The later version, in the *Recherche*, suggests a deeper disregard for appearances: 'not so much with the idea of appearing "dressed" in the eyes of the hotel staff as in order to appear to me to be less in mourning, less sad, almost consoled' (K III 639, P II 625).

5   All Venetian gondolas have been black since the passing of the sumptuary laws of the sixteenth century. And the use by Proust of the diminutive 'voilette' means that we can appreciate the connotations of a 'little sail'

behind the 'little veil' denoted, whereas 'un voile' would have more obviously clashed with 'une voile' and the association would have been less smooth.

6 And Proust himself said that the 'miracle of Racine' was that Racine managed to 'become a woman [. . .] in his tragedies' (cf. R. de Chantal, *Marcel Proust critique littéraire*, Montreal 1967, p. 410).

7 K. Yoshikawa, in *Etudes sur la genèse de 'La Prisonnière'*, chapter 5, shows how the mother becomes less important in the *Recherche* than in *Contre Sainte-Beuve*, as Albertine becomes more artistic and intelligent. (Yoshikawa 1977). And H. Bonnet, in *'Le Temps retrouvé* dans les Cahiers', notes how Proust's relationship with Agostinelli, and the latter's death in 1914, gave the impetus for a separate volume introducing Albertine (*A l'ombre des jeunes filles en fleurs*) and for the regrouping of some key passages which Proust had already written for *Le Temps retrouvé*, into *La Prisonnière* (the Vinteuil septet and the death of Bergotte) or *La Fugitive* (the publication of the *Figaro* article and the trip to Venice itself) (Bonnet, 1973, p. 160–1).

8 Cf. G. Peroccho, *La Confrérie des Saints Georges et Tryphon. Guide de l'Ecole San Giorgio degli Schiavoni*, Venice 1964, p. 46.

9 The eagle is the symbol of St John the Evangelist, and the presence of such a spiritual transposition of the earlier eagle motif shows Marcel working towards a new equilibrium *vis-à-vis* Albertine (K III 656, P III 641). She is definitively rehabilitated a few pages later when her figure is allowed a dignified status in memory alongside that of Marcel's mother in the Baptistery (K III 661, P III 646). It is interesting to see how deeply and finely Proust's symbolism here is rooted in iconographical knowledge. The image of an eagle on Venetian coins is rare, but nonetheless attested. A specially minted coin, distributed annually by the Doge, was called the 'osella' (the bird) because it replaced a tribute payable in wild fowl originally due. Although these coins usually had a winged lion as their motif, one Doge, Silvestro Valier (1694–1700), did use the bird motif of the eagle (coins of 1694 and 1695) and the dove (coin of 1699). Cf. G. Werdnig, *Die Osellen oder Münz-Medaillen der Republik Venedig*, Wien 1889. The connection with the Knights of St John is Proust's own idea.

10 *St Mark's Rest*, p. 26.

11 *St Mark's Rest*, pp. 8–9, 16–17.

12 A. Whittick (ed.), *Ruskin's Venice*, London 1976, pp. 161–3 (Tr. Ed. pp. 115–19). And my comparison of Ruskin's view of incrusted architecture with Proust's handling of quotation and illustration is authorised by Proust's own comment on Ruskin's style:

Every time that Ruskin, by way of quotation, but more often by way of allusion, incorporates into the structure of his sentences some biblical recollection, as the Venetians inserted in their monuments the sacred sculptures and precious stones they brought from the Orient, I have always looked up the exact reference so that the reader might see to what changes Ruskin would submit a verse before using it, and thus might better realize the mysterious yet unchanging chemistry of his mind, the originality and precision of his thought.

('Avant Propos à la Bible d'Amiens' (*ORR* 7, *CSB* P 729)).

13 'I have used the word duplicity in no depreciatory sense [...] this incrusted school [...] appears insincere at first to a Northern builder, because, accustomed to build with solid blocks of freestone, he is in the habit of supposing the external superficies of a piece of masonry to be some criterion of its thickness. But, as soon as he gets acquainted with the incrusted style, he will find that the Southern builders had no intention to deceive him. He will see that every slab of facial marble is fastened to the next by a confessed *rivet*, and that the joints of the armour are so visibly and openly accommodated to the contours of the substance within, that he has no more right to complain of treachery than a savage would have, who, for the first time in his life seeing a man in armour, had supposed him to be made of solid steel' (*The Stones of Venice*, Tr. Ed., pp. 117–18).

4. 'Superiore all 'invidia' – Proust's transpositions of Ruskin

1 J. Autret, *L'Influence de Ruskin sur la vie, les idées et l'œuvre de Marcel Proust*, Genève 1955; B. Bucknall, *The religion of Art in Proust*, Urbana, Illinois 1969; J.-Y. Tadié, *Proust et le roman*, Paris 1971. D. Ellison, *The Reading of Proust*, Oxford 1984.

2 Cf. L. Dällenbach, *Le Récit spéculaire*, Paris 1977, for a discussion of *mise en abîme*.

3 Cf. *ORR* 42, *CSB* P 121.

4 Cf. *A l'ombre des jeunes filles en fleurs* (K I 894–5, P I 836).

5 Cf. for instance K III 665, P III 650: 'After dinner, I went out alone, into the heart of the enchanted city where I found myself in the middle of strange purlieus like a character in the *Arabian Nights*.' The figure of the blue flower also recalls the image of the stained-glass window at St Hilaire in Combray, whose reflection on the floor of the church was described as: 'this dazzling, gilded carpet of forget-me-nots in glass' (K I 65, P I 60).

6 The image-cluster was already in an early draft: 'And the shadow cast by the draper's awning or the barber's pole was a mere darkening of the sapphire where the head of a bearded god is thrust from a palace doorway, or the little blue flower that the shadow of a delicate piece of carving prints on the sunny surface of a paved walk' (*BWSB* 65, *CSB* F 121).

7 '[...] since one had to take a gondola to go there, the church represented for me not simply a monument but the terminus of a voyage on these vernal, maritime waters, with which, I felt, St Mark's formed an indivisible and living whole. My mother and I would enter the baptistery (K III 660–1, P III 645–6).

8 Although Ruskin's 'church' is ultimately religious, and Proust's aesthetic. Proust actually uses the Noah's ark image when talking of Laon cathedral in *Le côté de Guermantes* (K II 7–8, P II 13), mentioning:

> a time when on the summit of the hill of Laon the nave of its cathedral had not yet been poised like the Ark of the Deluge on the summit of Mount Ararat, crowded with Patriarchs and Judges anxiously leaning from its windows to see whether the wrath of God has yet subsided [...].

9 (K III 728–36, P III 709–17).

10 (K III 729, P III 709–10).

11 Cf. G. Mariacher, *Il Sansovino*, Milano 1962, plates 31, 35.

12 Or imitation Rizzo, since the inner 'scala d'oro' is by Sansovino, and the outer 'scala dei giganti' is by Rizzo.

13 The Doge who commanded the decoration of the Baptistery, Andrea Dandolo, also has his tomb in the Baptistery (cf. my chapter 8).

14 (K I 42–4, 353, P I 40, 324).

15 In Proust's pastiche of Ruskin, 'La bénédiction du sanglier', Proust parodies Ruskin's mixture of galloping metaphor, obscure learning, and lush prose:

> While at his feet the dome of the Invalides offered up its form, then unique, but which, against the azure of the Grand Canal at Venice, would later espouse the eternal pallor of the church of Santa Maria della Salute, but without resembling her French mother any more than a crude snowball can pass itself off as the apple of the Hesperides, the church of the Sacred Heart at Montmartre, although hardly much older, offered up to the setting sun, as if in a basket, the symmetrical fructification of its blueish cupolas, for some of them to be covered with its orange glow.   (*CSB* P 203).

Thus Proust shows Ruskin's Salute and the Invalides participating in an over-complex conceit, as happily as he uses them himself as an example of the over-obvious.

16 Since Antonio Rizzo fled Venice in 1498 and died in the Marches in 1500, the bust of Leonardo Loredan (Doge 1501–21) is most likely to be a Proustian invention.

17 Although perhaps in the last analysis we may suspect that Proust's memory played a trick on him; the cheekbones and the eyebrows are so striking in the Bellini portrait . . .

18 They apparently corrected the translation of *The Bible of Amiens* at Quadri's cafe and ate 'granita' ices at Florian's, in addition to reading Ruskin's *Stones of Venice* in the Baptistery (which was the occasion for Proust to be 'étrangement ému, et comme soulevé d'extase'). Cf. Painter, I 269–71. The article mocked 'des Anglaises [. . .] qui croient devoir se pencher sur les chapiteaux de St Marc célébrés par Ruskin' (Painter, II 8). Cf. Ruskin: '[. . .] no one has ever believed a word I said, though the public have from the first done me the honour to praise my manner of saying it; and, as far as they found the things I spoke of amusing to themselves, they have deigned for a couple of days or so to look at them, helped always through the tedium of the business by due quantity of ices at Florian's, music by moonlight on the Grand Canal, paper-lamps, and the English papers and magazines at M. Ongaria's [. . .]' (*The Stones of Venice*, Tr. Ed., Orpington 1879–81, pp. 164–5).

5. Into the abyss: Bellini, Mantegna, Giotto

1 Whittick, p. 170. cf. Ruskin, *St. Mark's Rest*, p. 99: 'These mosaics [i.e., the ones in the Baptistery] are the only ones in the interior of the church which belong to the time (1204) when its façade was completed by the placing of the Greek horses over its central arch, and illumined by the lovely series of mosaics still represented in Gentile Bellini's pictures, of which one only now remains. That *one*, left nearly intact – as Fate has willed – represents the church itself so completed; and the bearing of the body of St Mark into its gates, with all the great kings and queens who have visited his shrine, standing to look on; not conceived, mind you, as present at any actual time, but as always looking on in their hearts.'

2 J. T. Johnson (p. 345). P. A. Spalding, and the editors of the Pléiade edition (1954), are less scrupulous.

3 From *The Relation between Michael Angelo and Tintoret*, 1872, pp. 14–15.

4 Whittick, p. 18 (*Guide to the Principal Pictures in the Academy of Fine Arts*).

5 Another Ruskin favourite (Whittick, p. 288).

6 Cf. J. M. Cocking, *Proust*, Cambridge 1982, p. 141–2.

7 Swann also rather simply likens Bloch to Gentile Bellini's *Mahomet II* because of his (semitic) facial features (K I 105, P I 97); and likens himself to Mahomet II on account of the latter's notorious jealousy (K I 386, P I 355).

8 In Swann's eyes, one of Mme de Saint-Euverte's valets looks like a Renaissance executioner; another resembles a bored soldier; others recall the statues on the 'Giants' staircase' at the Doges' Palace in Venice. Swann refers to Mantegna, but the *Pala di San Zeno* at Verona does not contain the *Massacre of the Innocents* mentioned. I suspect that Proust is conflating the crucifixion sequence of the *Pala di San Zeno* with the *Martyrdom of St James and St Christopher* frescoes in the Cappella Ovetari at the Chiesa degli Eremitani in Padua (whose statuesque soldiers and by-standers are admired by Swann), and transferring to them a reminiscence of Giotto's striking *Massacre of the Innocents* from his famous fresco sequence in the Cappella degli Scrovegni, which stands close by the Eremitani (K I 353, P I 323–4).

9 Another Mantegna painting, also in the Louvre, might have been in Proust's thoughts. This is a crucifixion from the *Predella dalla Pala di San Zeno*, which has a more obvious 'terraced city' in the background than the *San Sebastiano*, and, moreover, is referred to by Swann (K I 353, P I 323–4) – and see note 8, above).

10 The 'palais du Trocadéro' was built for the 'exposition universelle' of 1878 by Davioud and Bourdais. It had the style of a Roman amphitheatre, but was flanked by two rather incongruously tall, narrow and angular towers (cf. *Grand Larousse Encyclopédique*).

11 'abandon all hope' is a direct quotation from Canto III of the *Inferno*: 'Lasciate ogni speranza voi ch'entrate'. A few lines later Dante says that Virgil 'mi mise dentro alle segrete cose'. The 'pestiferous cavern' does not appear to be a direct quotation, but the whole of Dante's hell is this kind of foul lair. In Canto IV, for instance, Dante finds himself on the edge of the 'valle d'abisso dolorosa' which is 'Oscura, profond' [...] e nebolosa'. These underworld clouds, in Dante's inverted cone, may well have triggered Proust's vision of the railway cupola and its disturbingly falsely clouded heaven as a veritable hell. In Canto IX hell is 'Questa palude che il gran puzzo spira', there is 'fummo [...] acerbo' and 'nebbia folta'. In Canto X it is 'una valle [...] che infin lassu facea spiacer suo lezzo', and in Canto XI 'l'orribile soperchio del puzzo, che il profondo abisso gitta'. Proust's interest in and reflections of Dante have been studied by R. Bales (*Proust and the Middle Ages*), and S. Borton

('A tentative essay on Dante and Proust', *Revue de Littérature comparée*), but they do not seem to have noticed this particular concordance. Even Proust's transposition of the infernal depths to the technological heights arises naturally from Dante's Italian, where 'alta' means 'deep', yet is the etymological equivalent of the French 'haute' or 'high' (cf. Dante's '*alta* valle feda' of Canto XII, for example: 'the *deep*, fetid valley'.

12 'When my father had decided, one year, that we should go for the Easter holidays to Florence and Venice, not finding room to introduce into the name of Florence the elements that ordinarily constitute a town, I was obliged to evolve a supernatural city from the impregnation by certain vernal scents of what I supposed to be, in its essentials, the genius of Giotto. At most – and because one cannot make a name extend much further in time than in space – like some of Giotto's paintings themselves which show us at two separate moments the same person engaged in different actions, here lying in his bed, there getting ready to mount his horse, the name of Florence was divided into two compartments. In one, beneath an architectural canopy, I gazed at a fresco over which was partly drawn a curtain of morning sunlight, dusty, oblique and gradually spreading; in the other [...] I moved swiftly – the quicker to arrive at the lunch-table that was spread for me with fruit and a flask of Chianti – across a Ponte Vecchio heaped with jonquils, narcissi and anemones' (K I 423, P I 389–90).

13 Cf. Painter, II, 235, 239.

14 The dream also shows that the creativity sought by Marcel in the world in his waking hours lies in fact at the interface of reality and consciousness.

15 Proust's link between Venice and Dutch-style painting is more explicit in *Le Côté de Guermantes*, where a variant of the same passage appears – reviving Venetian structures in Paris:

> It is not only in Venice that one has these views on to several houses at once which have proved so tempting to painters; it is just the same in Paris. Nor do I cite Venice at random. It is of its poorer quarters that certain poor quarters of Paris remind one, in the morning, with their tall, splayed chimneys.

It is also quite possible that the conventional view of Amsterdam as 'the Venice of the North' is also at the back of Proust's mind, despite the 'screen' reference to Delft and Haarlem. The proliferation of girls being groomed behind glass in the pictorial fantasy reminds us that Albertine had been to Amsterdam, and that this had disturbed the narrator: the role of the young ladies on display in windows in Amsterdam is unambiguous. Here again, the *Côté de Guermantes* variant is perhaps more suggestive – but this does not justify Kilmartin's omission of the whole passage, in *La fugitive* ([K III 665], P III 650):

> And then the extreme proximity of the houses, with their windows looking across at one another over a common courtyard, makes of each casement the frame in which a cook sits dreamily gazing down at the ground below, or, further off, a girl is having her hair combed by an old woman with a witchlike face, barely distinguishable in the shadow: thus each courtyard provides the neighbours in the adjoining house, suppressing sound by its width and framing silent gestures in a series of rectangles placed under glass by the closing of the windows, with an exhibition of a hundred Dutch paintings hung in rows. (K II 594, P II 572).

16 This imaginary exhibition of Dutch paintings, where Marcel tries to come to grips with the nature of his consciousness and fantasy and reality, no doubt echoes the 'real' exhibition of Dutch paintings, where Bergotte died in the instant of feeling that his writing fails if measured against Vermeer's painting, only to be exonerated by the narrator (K III 184–6, III 186–7; cf. my chapter 8).

17 The link between the *Arabian Nights* and Venice is made quite spontaneously by Proust's fictitious Goncourt:

> their mansion, which its owner claims was once the mansion of the Venetian Ambassadors and in which there is a room used as a smoking-room which Verdurin tells me was transported lock, stock and barrel, as in a tale of the *Thousand and One Nights*, from a celebrated *palazzo* whose name I forget. (K III 729, P III 710).

6. Fortuny (I): A phoenix too frequent

1 *Immagine e materiali del laboratorio Fortuny*, ed. S. Fuso, Venezia 1978.

2 Cf. A. M. de Sanchez Rivero, *Quattro Spagnoli in Venezia*, Venezia 1957.

3 K. Yoshikawa in chapter 5 of *Etudes sur la genèse de La Prisonnière* (Paris 1977) says that the details concerning Fortuny were added in 1915–16. This is consistent with Proust's correspondence with Maria de Madrazo in 1916 ('Huit lettres inédites à Maria de Madrazo, prés. par M. Riefstahl-Nordlinger,' *BSAMP*, 3, 1953, p. 23–38.

4 J. M. Cocking attests Proust's interest in Réjane's costumes when he argues that the description of Elstir's painting of Odette is based on a photograph in Proust's possession of Réjane dressed as the Prince de Sagan (J. M. Cocking, *Proust*, Cambridge 1982, p. 149).

5 Painter, II, 288, 294.

6 And Ruskin had called this 'the best picture in the world' (*St. Mark's Rest*, p. 38).

7 In fact Tiepolo is mentioned in the *Recherche* only on the three occasions that a Fortuny dress recreates his reds or pinks (K II 686, P II 661; K II 745, P II 719; K III 401, P III 394).

8 Although for the record we should add that Oriane has dresses in 'black crêpe de Chine' and 'white taffeta' as well as 'blue velvet' (cf. J. Monnin-Hornung, *Proust et la peinture*, Genève 1951, p. 161). In a recent exhibition of clothes belonging to an early 20th-century opera singer, it was interesting to see that the two items designed by Fortuny were precisely such a black and a white dress: *Mostra: Il guardaroba di una cantante: vestiti e costumi del primo '900*. Elenco opere esposte nos. 23 & 24 (exhibition at Museo Fortuny, Venezia, 1983). However, Proust's use of this kind of simple little black or white dress transcends mere social observation. Albertine's 'black satin dress' is for Marcel a carefully calculated darkening of the celestial blue robe: 'we observe like a black sky the casual clothes she puts on when she is with us, keeping for other people the dresses with which she used to flatter us' (K III 98, P III 102–3).

9 The 'biblioteca Ambrosiana' is actually in Milan. Proust's mature writing usually concentrates metaphors in thematic groups through metonymic association (cf. P. J. Collier & J. Whiteley, 'Proust's blank page', *Modern Language Review*, July 1984). In order to remain within the Venetian context here Proust would have had to have referred to the 'biblioteca Marciana'. I am inclined to think that the intrusion of the 'Ambrosiana' is a lapsus. In an early draft of the Venetian material, Proust commits some quite rococo images to paper, mingling his impressions of St Mark's with those of modern exhibitions, Northern architecture, rococo bookbinding, eighteenth-century opera and classical tragedy:

> in Venice, when we see Saint Mark's for the first time our predominant impression will be of a broad squat building with Venetian masts, like an Exhibition pavilion; or at Jumièges, of the cathedral towers standing like giants in the forecourt of some genteel little property on the outskirts of Rouen; or at Saint-Wandrille, of the rococo binding of a romanesque missal, like a Rameau opera with its peruked and befeathered treatment of a classical theme.
>
> (*BWSB* 181, *CSB* F 284).

The interpenetration of two styles – Renaissance and Oriental – is much more subtly operated in the text of the *Recherche* (where it also subsumes the interpenetration of the Fortuny and Carpaccio imagery).

10 As J. Y. Tadié says in *Proust et le roman*, Paris 1971, the dresses become a decor and Albertine 'a device for suggesting Venice' (p. 97).

11 Proust does not seem to have started out with the preconception that the painter had to be Carpaccio: 'do you also know whether there are any paintings in Venice (I'd like some titles) with coats or dresses that Fortuny is supposed to have (or could have) been inspired by? I'd look out reproductions of the pictures and I'd see if I could be inspired by them myself' ('Huit lettres inédites à Maria de Madrazo', p. 31). But he resists offers by Madame Straus and Maria de Madrazo to show him a *real* Fortuny coat, and clearly feels that his memory of Carpaccio paintings seen sixteen years previously and commemorated in black-and-white reproductions, and second-degree documentation on Carpaccio and Fortuny, are preferable to the real garment, which he twice rejects: 'Madame Straus wanted to lend me a coat (which must be like yours according to what you have told me about yours) but I don't need it, and likewise I decline your offer to show me yours. There would be no point. I have already seen one or two [...]. What would be most useful for my purposes would be if there were a book *on* Fortuny (or articles written by him) if you could let me know the title [...]. Otherwise any precise details about a particular dress or coat (did he never create *shoes?*) in a particular Carpaccio painting. Carpaccio happens to be a painter I know very well, I spent days at San Giorgio Degli Schiavoni, and days looking at St Ursula, I have translated everything Ruskin ever wrote about each of these paintings, everything etc. As far as my novel is concerned, another Venetian or even Paduan painter would have been easier. But I never let a day go by without looking at reproductions of Carpaccio paintings, so I will be on home ground' (pp. 34–5). Proust is obviously preparing to recreate his *own* Fortuny dresses, using thematic and emblematic transposition. Cf. also below, n. 10 to ch. 7.

12 Whittick, p. 277.

13 Whittick, p. 277.

14 Morris/Ruskin, pp. 82, 113.

15 Cf. Ruskin's illustration, *Stones of Venice*, London 1851–6, vol. II, ch. v, plate XI (reproduced on p. 86). It is symptomatic of Proust's debt to Ruskin that we find Ruskin explaining that peacocks drinking out of fountains are symbolic of resurrection, and that peacocks drinking out of fonts are symbolic of the new life given through baptism (*SV*, II, V, para XXX, pp. 143–4). Ruskin makes no mention of phoenixes, either here or even in his *General Index*, London 1886 – yet another

reason to suppose that Proust's symbolic bird of resurrection is above all the peacock.

16 As the image of light on the floor evoking glass forget-me-nots looks forward to the shadows in the form of blue flowers cast on the stones of St Mark's square in Venice.

17 L. Price, 'Bird imagery surrounding Proust's Albertine', *Symposium*, 26, no. 3, Fall 1972, pp. 242–59 (p. 255). D. de Agostini, 'Albertine: "figura allegorica" dell'opera, "metafora" della scrittura', in *Una Idea di "Recherche", Aut Aut*, nuova seria no. 193–4, genn.–aprile 1983, pp. 43–61 (p. 60).

18 Although paradoxically the medium of this regeneration will be revealed in *Le Temps retrouvé* to be sensory rather than intellectual.

19 Proust had apparently chosen this motif for its symbolic power *before* checking whether Fortuny actually used it. He writes to Maria de Madrazo: 'Do you know [...] whether Fortuny ever used for his dressing gowns the motif of those mating birds, drinking out of a vase for example, which are so common at St Mark's, on the Byzantine capitals?' ('Huit lettres inédites à Maria de Madrazo') *BSAMP*, 3, 1953, 31. And Proust intended the symbolism to be erotically charged: 'The very brief description of these dresses illustrates our love scenes (and that is why I prefer dressing gowns because she is in my bedroom in her 'déshabillé', a glamorous one, but nonetheless a 'déshabillé')' (ibid., p. 34).

20 Cf. my note 14.

7. *Fortuny (II): Carpaccio's material*

1 *BWSB* 180, *CSB* F 283. A hotel dining room is likened to 'the bedroom in the *Dream of Saint Ursula*'.

2 And Carpaccio's paintings are at least as persuasive a model for this composite painting of Elstir's as are the various Impressionist sources cited by most critics. J. M. Cocking notes that Elstir's painting looks out from the shore towards the sea (*Proust*, Cambridge 1982, p. 148). This is also true, of course, of Carpaccio's St Ursula sequence.

3 It is interesting to note that as early as the first draft of *Combray* Proust was already preparing us for this motif: 'The curé also mentions a 16th-century Persian carpet, but the narrator does not pay attention', notes C. Quémar, 'L'Eglise de Combray, son curé et le narrateur', *Cahiers Marcel Proust* (nouvelle série), 6, re. Proust's Cahier 6 (Fol 3rO).

4 C. Robin identifies Memling's 'panels from the reliquary at Bruges' in the musée de l'Hôpital Saint-Jean. ('Le retable de la cathédrale', *Cahiers Marcel Proust* (n.s.), 9, (*Etudes Proustiennes* III), p. 83). Memling's reliqu-

ary is also on St Ursula. I prefer to see Proust's allusion as mainly inspired by a freely interpreted Carpaccian structure.

5 Proust may have remembered Ruskin on the *Arrival of the Ambassadors*, where Ursula is standing before her father 'in a plain housewifely dress' (Clegg p. 150, Ruskin XXVII 347, *Fors* letter 20, 'Benediction'); although in Ruskin's version it is the father who is unhappy at the impending marriage, rather than Ursula upset at her advances being rejected.

6 Cf. (*ORR* 52, *CSB* P 132), for Proust's direct translation (in his PS to the *Bible d'Amiens*) of Ruskin's Stones of Venice: 'through century after century of gathering vanity and fostering guilt, that white dome of St Mark's had uttered in the dead ear of Venice, "Know thou, that for all these things God will bring thee into judgment"' [Cf. Ecclesiastes 11:9] [*The Stones of Venice, CW* 10:141–2].

7 G. Peroccho, *La Confrérie des Saints Georges et Tryphon. Guide de l'Ecole San Giorgio degli Schiavoni*, Venezia 1964, p. 23.

8 Autret notes this in relation to the oriental motifs commented by Elstir at Balbec. I claim responsibility for relating it to Fortuny etc.

9 Proust actually read part of the text of Mâle's *L'Art religieux du XIIe siècle en France* in *La Revue de Paris*, in 1921. And Proust kept in close touch with Emile Mâle and his writing from 1904 until 1921, so that it is likely that he would have been aware of any new insight of Mâle's, before its final appearance in print. (See R. Bales, *Proust and the Middle Ages*, Genève 1975, pp. 28–31, and R. de Billy, *Marcel Proust: Lettres et conversations*, Paris 1930, pp. 118–20, and R. Bales, 'Proust et Emile Mâle', *BSAMP*, 24, 1974, pp. 1925–36.)

10 And this inversion of the mirroring process was intended by Proust from the outset of his Fortuny/Carpaccio draft, as far as one can tell from his correspondence with Maria de Madrazo: '[...] a long time afterwards, after much suffering, followed by a period where I more or less forget her, I go to Venice, but in a painting by XXX (let's say Carpaccio, since you say that Fortuny was inspired by *Carpaccio*), I recognise a dress that I had given her. Previously this dress had conjured up Venice for me and made me long to leave Albertine, now the Carpaccio where I see it conjures up Albertine for me, and makes Venice painful to bear' ('Huit lettres inédites à Maria de Madrazo, *BSAMP*, 3, 1953, p. 34). Maria sent him a reproduction of Carpaccio's *Miracle of the Holy Cross* (cf. ibid., p. 36) (also known as the *Patriarch of Grado*), since Proust had asked: 'As for Fortuny I would really like to know which Carpaccio paintings inspired him or could have inspired him, and in these Carpaccio paintings, which dress exactly, and in what way [...]' (ibid., p. 33). Despite Proust's detailed questioning ('it's the character

with his back turned, isn't it?' (p. 37)), he makes Albertine's coat blue, whereas the Compagno della Calza's cloak is red (K III 412, 419; P III 405, 412). J. T. Johnson argues that the colour of Albertine's cape was influenced by the blue of the sky (*The Painter and his Art in the Works of Marcel Proust*, Wisconsin 1964, p. 159). One might add that the colours of Albertine's Fortuny dresses are necessarily the blue and gold of the sunlit Grand Canal, whatever colours Carpaccio may have used ... Proust's problem is also that black-and-white reproduction gives no indication of colour, and that he is more familiar with the St Ursula sequence: 'As for the Compagni della Calza I remember them better in the Life of St Ursula [...] But I don't have the painting clear enough in my mind's eye to remember the colours. So when you see Fortuny you would do me a great favour if you would ask him for the most technical description of his coat, as if it were for a catalogue, noting the material, colours, pattern (it's the character with his back turned, isn't it?)' (p. 37). The painting from the St Ursula cycle with conspicuous Compagni della Calza is no doubt the *Return of the English Ambassadors*. This painting, too, has a foreground figure presenting a sumptuously cloaked back). These letters all date from 1916.

11 'I enjoyed watching the glass jars which the village boys used to lower into the Vivonne to catch minnows, and which, filled by the stream, in which they in their turn were enclosed, at once "containers" whose transparent sides were like solidified water and "contents" plunged into a still larger container of liquid, flowing crystal, conjured up an image of coolness more delicious and more provoking than they would have done standing upon a table laid for dinner, by showing it as perpetually in flight between the impalpable water in which my hands could not grasp it and the insoluble glass in which my palate could not enjoy it' (K I 183–4, P I 168).

8. Born again: Marcel's mosaic

1 It fails to merit mention for instance among Howard Moss's *eighteen* occasions when a significant act of memory or suchlike occurs: H. Moss, *The Magic Lantern of Marcel Proust*, New York 1962. It does not appear in Milton Hindus's summary of the Venetian section of *La Fugitive*: M. Hindus, *A Reader's Guide to Marcel Proust*, London 1962. It is not one of Roger Shattuck's *eleven* 'Privileged moments': R. Shattuck, *Proust's Binoculars*, London 1963.

2 L. Bolle, *Marcel Proust ou le complexe d'Argus*, pp. 80–1, 84, 94–5.

3 G. Genette, *Figures* III, Paris 1972, pp. 48–9. Genette speaks of the

mosaique du baptême, "en rapport avec le site", où le Jourdain présente comme un second baptistère *en abyme* à l'intérieur du premier'.

4 J.-P. Richard, *Proust et le monde sensible*, Paris 1974, pp. 161–3, 171–4.

5 Ruskin – 'the Book-Temple' (*The Stones of Venice*, ed. Morris, p. 97). This is noted by Proust in a long quotation from *The Stones* in 'En mémoire des églises assassinées, III John Ruskin' (*ORR* 51–2, *CSB* P 131).

6 J.-P. Richard, *Proust et le monde sensible*, Paris 1974, pp. 174–5. Autret quotes *La Bible d'Amiens*: 'it is none the less in order to try to see what those "Old eyes" had seen that we went every day to shut ourselves away inside the dark and dazzling baptistery. And we could say of Ruskin as Ruskin said of Turner: "It is through those long-dead eyes that generations not yet born will see their colours".' J. Autret, *L'influence de Ruskin sur la vie, les idées et l'œuvre de Marcel Proust*, Genève 1955, p. 177. And in Proust's review of 'John Ruskin: Les Pierres de Venise. Trad. par Mme Mathilde P. Crémieux', he says how he sought the sights described by Ruskin and coloured in advance by Ruskin's prose: 'Our pilgrims' passion for stones which had started as thoughts and became thoughts again for us, led us to hear such admirable prayers by the Master beside the waters! To the colours of the heavens of Venice, of the mosaics of St Mark's, will be added new colours, more prestigious even because they are the very shades of a marvellous imagination, the colours of Ruskin, which in his prose, like an enchanted vessel, sail round the world!' (*CSB* P 521–2).

7 J.-P. Richard, op. cit., p. 204.

8 Her celebration of sorbets, which wittily pastiches his style, shows how well – too well, no doubt – she has learnt her lesson (K III 125–7, P III 129–31); her comment on a Mantegna painting shows that she can foreground a minor, anachronistic detail as slickly as Swann or Marcel (K III 165, P III 168).

9 I am grateful to Professor Malcolm Bowie for making this point in his *Freud, Proust and Lacan*, Cambridge 1987, pp. 85–8. Art historians tell us that the personage is actually Ursula's nurse.

10 We have already seen that in *La Fugitive* Marcel's allusions to *Phèdre* suggest transposition of gender (cf. chapter 3).

11 And perhaps it might be appropriate here to evoke Proust's mother's probable wishful thinking about the marriageable English girl Marie Nordlinger.

12 The mother is the medium of artistic initiation in an early draft: 'After the train had left ... and before we reached Venice, Mamma read me

that dazzling passage in which Ruskin successively compares it to a coral reef in the Indian seas and to an opal.' (*BWSB* 66, *CSB* F 122).

13 Whittick, p. 276.

14 Earlier in 'En mémoire des églises assassinées, III John Ruskin', Proust had ascribed to Ruskin the ability to resurrect through art:

It is a single thought of the sculptor, in fact, that has been arrested here in its movement by the immobility of the stone. [...] nothing therefore dies that has survived, no more the sculptor's thought than Ruskin's thought [...] At the call of the angel, each corpse will be found still there, in his place, when we believed him dust long ago.   (*ORR* 46–7, *CSB* P 126–7).

But it is interesting to see how already in referring to Ruskin Proust had seen the resuscitation as a regressive structure: the sculptor resurrects a real person by reproducing him in stone; Ruskin resurrects the sculptor's genius by his own descriptive genius; Proust (and companions) through a mixture of viewing and reading resurrect Ruskin, sculptor and personage. And in *Le Temps retrouvé* we will find an echo of this view that artistic creation is more an act of reading than of writing, and that it constitutes a kind of Last Judgement:

As for the inner book of unknown symbols (symbols carved in relief they might have been, which my attention, as it explored my unconscious, groped for and stumbled against and followed the contours of, like a diver exploring the ocean-bed), if I tried to read them no one could help me with any rules, for to read them was an act of creation in which no one can do our work for us or even collaborate with us. How many for this reason turn aside from writing! [...] But excuses have no place in art and intentions count for nothing: at every moment the artist has to listen to his instinct, and it is this that makes art the most real of all things, the most austere school of life, the true last judgment.

(K III 913–14, P III 879–80).

15 The sculpture, we have seen (cf. n. 14) has to be resurrected through the creative reading operated by the viewer – which implies his own ability to revive former selves, an ability which Marcel has not yet mastered: 'I should have been incapable of resuscitating Albertine because I was incapable of resuscitating myself, of resuscitating the self of those days.' (K III 657, P III 642).

16 Again we should notice the idea of salvation through narrative in the reference to the *Arabian Nights*, and note the regressive structuring: Albertine within a miniature Venetian mental prison formed by Marcel's mind, whilst Marcel himself is within Venice. Cf. also ch. 2.

17 Perhaps she in her turn is to be held in the 'piombi' or lead strips of a stained-glass window, like the sea in *A l'ombre des jeunes filles en fleurs:* then, in the greenish glass which it distended with the curve of its rounded waves, the sea, set between the iron uprights of my casement window like a piece of stained glass in its leads, ravelled out over all the deep rocky border of the bay little plumed triangles of motionless foam etched with the delicacy of a feather of a downy breast from Pisanello's pencil, and fixed in that white, unvarying, creamy enamel which is used to depict fallen snow in Gallé's glass.

(K I 860, P II 802–3).

18 The reference to Marcel's notebook on Ruskin in the Baptistery is an addition to the typescript, and therefore a significant feature, rather than some circumstantial or autobiographical detail. (Cf. R. Bales, *Proust and the Middle Ages*, Genève 1975, p. 72.)

19 Cf. P. J. Collier & J. Whiteley, 'Proust's Blank Page', *Modern Language Review*, July 1984.

20 Genette speaks of the 'hieratic immobility of the maternal image in the memory of the "sanctuary"', like that of one of the mosaic images facing her' (*Figures* III, p. 49). It would be even more appropriate to interchange Genette's terms and speak of 'the sanctuary of memory'. Marcel sanctifies his mother's figure by formalising it within the mosaic framework of memory and art.

21 Ruskin says of the Madonna of S. Donato (Murano): 'The figure wears a robe of blue, deeply fringed with gold' (*Whittick*, p. 57).

22 The traditional redemption of erotic desire through maternal love, figured in the reconciliation at the foot of the cross between Mary Magdalene and the Virgin Mary. The inscription around the inside of the dome of S. Donato reads: 'Quos Eva contrivit, pia virgo Maria redemit' (*Whittick*, p. 57).

23 In 'Journées de lecture', a version of his preface to his own translation of Ruskin's *Sesame and Lilies*, Proust had already used the Theodore/ Mark model regressively within his central image of Venice containing the past within the present:

How many times, in *The Divine Comedy*, in Shakespeare, have I known that impression of having before me, inserted into the present actual hour, a little of the past, that dreamlike impression which one experiences in Venice on the Piazzetta, before its two columns of gray and pink granite that support on their Greek capitals, one the Lion of Saint Mark, the other Saint Theodore trampling the crocodile under his feet – beautiful strangers come from the Orient over the sea at which they gaze in the distance and which comes to die at their feet, and who both, without understanding the conversations going on around them in a language which is not that of their country, on this public square where their heedless smile still shines, keep on prolonging in our midst their days of the twelfth century, which they interpose in our today.

(*ORR* 128, *CSB* P 194).

24 In *Jean Santeuil* the problem of maternal passions is no doubt symbolised in Jean's angry smashing of a piece of Venetian glassware which was a present from his mother ('the Venetian glass which his mother had bought him for a hundred francs, and which he had just smashed' (*JS* 418; J.-P. Richard p. 56)). I would add to Richard's insight a point more germane to my own interpretation – that the mosaic could then easily be interpreted as a reconstruction of the broken fragments of glass, a reparation of the transgression and a reconstruction of filial love.

25 Although Proust has already signalled Ruskinian study as a means towards creativity: 'And now Ruskin will help lead us away from this rather passive contemplation of Venice [...] what inexhaustible and marvellous information Venice will offer us, now that Ruskin will make its very stones speak, and, thanks to Mme Crémieux's translation, speak to us in our own language, like one of those Apostles inspired with the gift of tongues, whose image we see on the baptistery of St Mark's! [...] now that we have returned from our Ruskinian pilgrimage, which was full of painstaking activity, now that we will seek truth rather than pleasure, the pleasure will be all the greater, and Venice will pour forth the greater enchantment for having been for us a place of study and for offering bliss as a supplement' (*CSB* P 521–2). Which book review of Mme Crémieux's translation of *The Stones of Venice* already shows the regressive, layering process at work. Proust's study of Mme Crémieux's translation of Ruskin's study of St Mark's nonetheless shows in a brilliant image how an apparently regressive text – the cartoon-like caption of a mosaic apostle's speech – in fact bursts out from its illustrative confines and stands for the whole creative power of the falsely modest artist-apostle: Proust. Swann with his idolatry, and Marcel's grandmother with her layers of art, are not so much wrong, as not ruthless enough in their pursuit of their own creative urges half-perceived within the borrowed forms of other artists.

26 Ruskin explains that according to an Italian chronicle, St Mark heard a voice saying to him 'Pax tibi Marce', telling him to rest at the lagoon, and build a stupendous city (*The Stones of Venice*, vol. II, ch. IV, para. II).

27 Bergotte's insight into the power of texture to furnish salvation may not be fortuitous in its choice of a 'petit ⌐pan de mur jaune'. Marcel in the Baptistery also comes face to face with the suddenly creative structuring of the golden patch of wall – in his case, the crystalline mosaic.

28 Cf. ch. 5 above for Marcel's own experience of this.

29 For Proust too it was the paintings of Carpaccio that made San Giorgio degli Schiavoni important (cf. his review of Mme M. P. Crémieux's translation of *The Stones of Venice, CSB* P 523).

30 This reading – different from that of the Pléiade and the Kilmartin editions which read 'amour' (love) for 'oeuvre' (work) – is that of Alison Winton, *Proust's Additions*, Cambridge 1977, since adopted by J. Milly in his edition of *La Prisonnière*, Flammarion 1984, p. 469. However, Milly sees the allegory as indicating a temporary freezing of Marcel's talent as long as he desires Albertine, rather than the prefiguration of mosaic structuring that I see in it:

> If 'œuvre' is the right reading, the parallel between 'ma mort' [my death] and 'mon œuvre' [my work] gives us to understand that Albertine asleep in the posture of the corpse is an allegory of the death of her friend's literary scruples.

(Milly, op. cit., p. 542, note 120).

31 The linking factor of memory, holding the figure of reconciled desire within the structure of mosaic artistry, was already foreshadowed in Proust's article on Nerval, where emotional experience was shown as having the power to take shape as it were in coloured stone within the mind's inner caverns:

> Telles sont ces matinées bénies, creusées (par une insomnie, l'ébranlement nerveux d'un voyage, une ivresse physique, une circonstance exceptionnelle) dans la dure pierre de nos journées, et gardant miraculeusement les couleurs délicieuses, exaltées, le charme de rêve qui les isole dans notre souvenir comme une grotte merveilleuse, magique et multicolore dans son atmosphère spéciale.

> Such are the blessed mornings that a sleepless night, the tossed nerves of a journey, a physical intoxication, some event out of the common, will hollow out for us in the hard rock of our daily lives, mornings that miraculously retain the delicious, feverish colours and dreamlike charm which sets them apart in our memory like an Aladdin's cave, magical and prismatic in an atmosphere all its own. (*BWSB* 116, *CSB* P 239).

The greater artistic maturity of the Baptistery scene is characterised by the way in which Proust transcends metaphor so that the Baptistery mosaics and the remembered figure of the mother have equal status, each an emblem of the other.

Bibliography

Works by Proust

A la Recherche du temps perdu, éd. P. Clarac & A. Ferré, Vols. I, II, III, Paris 1954 ('Bibliothèque de la Pléiade').

Contre Sainte-Beuve, suivi de Nouveaux mélanges, ed. B. de Fallois, Paris 1954.

Contre Sainte-Beuve, précédé de Pastiches et mélanges et suivi de Essais et articles, éd. P. Clarac & Y. Sandré, Paris 1971 (Pléiade).

Jean Santeuil, précédé de Les Plaisirs et les jours, ed. P. Clarac & Y. Sandré, Paris 1971 (Pléiade).

Correspondance, éd. P. Kolb, vol. I (1880–95), Paris 1970; vol. II (1896–1901), Paris 1976; vol. III (1902–3), Paris 1976.

Lettres à une amie, éd. M. Riefstahl-Nordlinger, Manchester 1942.

'Huit lettres inédites à Marie de Madrazo', prés. par M. Riefstahl-Nordlinger, *BSAMP*, 3, 1953, p. 23–38.

Textes retrouvés, éd. P. Kolb, *Cahiers Marcel Proust* (nouvelle série), 3, 1971.

Le Carnet de 1908, éd. P. Kolb, Cahiers Marcel Proust (n.s.), 8, 1976.

Translations

Remembrance of Things Past, Translated by C. K. Scott Moncrieff and Terence Kilmartin, Vols. 1, 2, 3, London 1983 ('Penguin Modern Classics').

On Reading Ruskin. Prefaces to *La Bible d'Amiens* and *Sésame et les lys*, with Selections from the Notes to the Translated Texts. Translated and Edited by Jean Autret, William Burford and Phillip J. Wolfe. With an Introduction by Richard Macksey, Yale University Press, New Haven and London 1987.

By Way of Sainte-Beuve. Translated by Sylvia Townsend-Warner. The Hogarth Press, New Edition with an Introduction by Terence Kilmartin, London 1984.

Bibliography

Books on Proust or with chapters on Proust

Autret, J. *L'influence de Ruskin sur la vie, les idées et l'œuvre de Marcel Proust*, Genève 1955.

Bales, R. *Proust and the Middle Ages*, Genève 1975.

Bardèche, M. *Marcel Proust romancier*, 2 vols., Paris 1971.

Bataille, G. *La Littérature et le mal*, Paris 1957.

Bell, W. S. *Proust's Nocturnal Muse*, New York 1962.

Benjamin, W. *Illuminations*, London 1973.

Beretta Anguissola, A. *Proust inattuale*, Roma 1976.

Bersani, L. *Marcel Proust: the Fictions of Life and Art*, New York 1965.

Bolle, L. *Marcel Proust ou le complexe d'Argus*, Paris 1967.

Bongiovanni Bertini, M. *Redenzione e metafora. Una lettura di Proust*, Milano 1981.

Bonnet, H. *Le progrès spirituel dans 'La recherche' de Marcel Proust*, 2e. éd. revue et augmentée, Paris 1979.

Bowie, M. *Freud, Proust and Lacan*, Cambridge 1987.

Boyer, P. *Le petit pan de mur jaune*, Paris 1987.

Brée, G. *Du Temps perdu au temps retrouvé*, Paris 1950.

Bucknall, B. *The Religion of Art in Proust*, Urbana, Ill. 1969.

Butor, M. *Les Œuvres d'art imaginaires chez Proust*, London 1964.

Caseaux, J. *L'Ecriture de Proust ou l'art du vitrail*, Paris 1971.

de Chantal, R. *Marcel Proust critique littéraire*, Montréal 1967.

Chernowitz, M. E. *Proust and painting*, New York 1944.

Cocking, J. M. *Proust*, Cambridge 1982.

Coleman, E. *The Golden Angel*, New York 1954.

Crosman, I. K. *Metaphoric Narration: the Structure and Function of Metaphor in A la recherche du temps perdu*, Chapel Hill 1978.

Curtius, E. R. *Marcel Proust*, Bologna 1984.

Daniel, G. *Temps et mystification dans A la recherche du temps perdu*, Paris 1963.

Deleuze, G. *Proust et les signes*, 4e. éd. remaniée, Paris 1976.

de Man, P. *Allegories of reading*, New Haven 1979.

Descombes, V. *Proust: philosophie du roman*, Paris 1987.

Ellison, D. *The Reading of Proust*, Oxford 1984.

Favrichon, A. *Toilettes et silhouettes féminines chez Marcel Proust*, Lyon 1987.

Festa-McCormick, D. *Proustian Optics of Clothes, Mirrors, Masks, Mores*, Stanford 1984.

Fiser, E. *L'Esthétique de Marcel Proust*, Paris 1933.

Genette, G. *Figures* III, Paris 1972.

Genette, G. & Todorov, T. (eds.), *Recherche de Proust*, Paris 1980.

Graham, V. *The Imagery of Proust*, Oxford 1966.

Bibliography

Green, F. C. *The Mind of Proust*, Cambridge 1949.

Guaraldo, E. *Lo specchio della differenza. Proust e la poetica della Recherche*, Roma 1977.

Henry, A. *Marcel Proust: théories pour une esthétique*, Paris 1981.

Proust romancier: le tombeau égyptien, Paris 1983.

Hindus, M. *The Proustian Vision*, New York 1954.

A Reader's Guide to Marcel Proust, London 1962.

Hughes, E. *Marcel Proust: a Study in the Quality of Awareness*, Cambridge 1983.

Hunt, J. D. & Holland, F. M. (eds.), *The Ruskin Polygon*, Manchester 1982.

Jackson, E. R. *L'Evolution de la mémoire involontaire dans l'œuvre de Marcel Proust*, Paris 1966.

Johnson, J. T. *The Painter and his Art in the Works of Marcel Proust* (dissertation), Wisconsin 1964.

Kilmartin, T. *A Guide to Proust*, London 1985.

Magnani, L. *La musica, il tempo, l'eterno nella Recherche di Proust*, Milano 1967.

Marcel Proust 1871–1922 (Whitworth Art Gallery). Manchester 1956.

Mendelson, D. *Le Verre et les objets de verre dans l'œuvre de Marcel Proust*, Paris 1968.

Milly, J. *Les Pastiches de Proust*, Paris 1970.

Monnin-Hornung, J. *Proust et la peinture*, Genève 1951.

Moss, H. *The Magic Lantern of Marcel Proust*, London 1963.

Newman-Gordon, P. *Dictionnaire des Idées dans l'œuvre de Proust*, The Hague 1968.

Oppici, P. *Proust e il movimento immobile*, 1983.

Painter, G. *Marcel Proust. A Biography*, vol. I, London 1959; vol. II, London 1965.

Poulet, G. *Etudes sur le temps humain*, I, Paris 1949.

L'Espace proustien, Paris 1963.

Price, L. B. (ed.), *Marcel Proust a Critical Panorama*, Urbana, Ill. 1973.

Proustiana (Atti del convegno internazionale di studi sull'opera di Marcel Proust), Padova 1973.

Richard, J. P. *Proust et le monde sensible*, Paris 1974.

Segal, N. *The Banal Object*, London 1981.

Shattuck, R. *Proust's Binoculars*, London 1964.

Sommella, P. P. *La moda nell' opera di Marcel Proust*, Rome 1986.

Spalding, P. A. *A Reader's Handbook to Proust*, London 1975.

Spitzer, L. *Marcel Proust e altri saggi di letteratura francese moderna*, Torino 1959.

Bibliography

Strauss, W. A. *Proust and Literature: the Novelist as Critic*, Cambridge, Mass. 1957.

Tadié, J.-Y. *Lectures de Proust*, Paris 1971.

Proust et le roman, Paris 1971.

Ullmann, S. *The Image in the Modern French Novel*, Cambridge 1960.

Una idea di 'Recherche', (*Aut Aut* nuova seria 193–194), Milano genn.–aprile 1983.

Ushiba, A. *L'Image de l'eau dans A la recherche du temps perdu*, Tokyo 1979.

Winton, A. *Proust's Additions*, 2 vols, Cambridge 1977.

Yoshikawa, K. *Etudes sur la genèse de La prisonnière*, Paris 1977.

Articles on Proust

Bailey, N. 'Symbolisme et composition dans l'œuvre de Proust', *French Studies*, XX no. 3, July 1966, pp. 253–66.

Bales, R. 'Proust & Emile Mâle', BSAMP, 24, 1974, pp. 1925–36.

Black, C. J. 'Albertine as an allegorical figure of time', *Romanic Review*, 54, Oct 1963, pp. 171–86.

Bonnet, H. '*Le Temps retrouvé* dans les Cahiers', *Cahiers Marcel Proust* (n.s.), 6 (*Etudes Proustiennes*, I), 1973, pp. 111–62.

Borton, S. 'A tentative essay on Dante and Proust', *Delaware Notes*, XXXI, 1958, pp. 33–42.

Bowie, M. 'Proust's Carpaccio' (paper read to Cambridge University Modern Languages Society), Cambridge 14 Jan 1983.

Chaix-Ruy, J. 'Marcel Proust et l'Italie', *Revue de Littérature Comparée*, XXIII, no. 4, oct-déc 1949, pp. 507–40.

Clogenson, Y. 'Le Thème de la cathédrale dans Proust', *BSAMP*, 14, 1964, pp. 152–9.

Collier, P. J. & Whiteley, J. 'Proust's Blank Page', *Modern Language Review*, July 1984, vol. 79, no. 3, pp. 570–8.

Comolli, G. 'Il messaggio della salvezza', *Una Idea di 'Recherche'*, *Aut Aut* nuova seria, Milano genn.–aprile 1983, pp. 83–96.

de Agostini, D. 'Albertine: "figura allegorica" dell'opera, "metafora" della scrittura', in *Una Idea di 'Recherche'*, *Aut Aut*, nuova seria, No. 193–4, Milano genn.–aprile 1983, pp. 43–61.

Dujardin, M. 'Marcel Proust à Venise', *Le Figaro*, 10 oct. 1932, p. 7.

Handler, L. 'Hommage à Mme Réjane', *Cahiers Marcel Proust* (n.s.), 3, 1971, pp. 324–5.

Iwasaka, T. 'Marcel Proust et l'Italie', *Etudes de Langue et de Littérature françaises*, no. 4, mars 1964, pp. 78–92.

Jacquillard, P. 'Proust et la peinture', *BSAMP*, 9, 1959, pp. 126–33.

Bibliography

Johnson, J. T. 'Marcel Proust et Gustave Moreau', *BSAMP*, 28, 1978, pp. 614–39.

Kawanago, H. '*Contre Sainte-Beuve* et la réminiscence dans "Venise"', *BSAMP*, 28, 1978, pp. 706–12.

Macksey, R. A. 'Proust on the margins of Ruskin', in J. D. Hunt & F. M. Holland (eds.), *The Ruskin Polygon*, Manchester 1982, pp. 172–97.

Price, L. B. 'Bird imagery surrounding Proust's Albertine', *Symposium*, 26, no. 3, Fall 1972, pp. 242–59.

Pugh, A. 'Le Séjour à Venise', *BSAMP*, 9, 1959, pp. 29–43.

Quémar, C. 'L'Eglise de Combray, son curé et son narrateur', *Cahiers Marcel Proust* (n.s.), 6, (*Etudes Proustiennes*, III), pp. 67–93.

Schoenfeld, J. S. 'Rôle des vêtements et de la mode dans *La Recherche*', *BSAMP*, 27, 1977, pp. 490–2.

Védrines, L. 'Séjours vénitiens', *BSAMP*, 4, 1954, pp. 57–60.

Yoshikawa, K. 'Genèse du leit-motiv Fortuny dans *A la recherche du temps perdu*', in *Etudes de langue et littérature française* 32, Tokyo 1978, pp. 102–20.

'Vinteuil ou la genèse du septuor', *Cahiers Marcel Proust* (n.s.), 9, 1979, (*Etudes Proustiennes*, III), pp. 287–347.

Other works consulted

Allen, G. *An Account of the Mosaics in the Baptistery of St. Mark's*, London 1884.

Birbari, E. *Dress in Italian Painting 1460–1500*, London 1975.

Braunstein, P. & Delort, R. *Venise: portrait historique d'une cité*, Paris 1971.

Calkins, R. G. *Monuments of Medieval Art*, Oxford 1979.

Cangogni, M. *L'Opera completa del Carpaccio*, Milano 1967.

Clegg, J. *Ruskin and Venice*, London 1981.

Cooper, J. G. *An Illustrated Encyclopaedia of Traditional Symbols*, London 1978.

Dällenbach, L. *Le Récit spéculaire*, Paris 1977.

Dante, *Enfer* (ed. A. Masseron), Paris 1954.

Fuso, S. (ed.), *Immagini e materiali del laboratorio Fortuny*, Venezia 1978.

Ghiotto, R. *L'Opera completa di Giovanni Bellini*, Milano 1969.

Goethe, J. W. von *Italian Journey*, London 1970.

Jacobus de Voragine *The Golden Legend* (tr. W. Caxton), London 1900.

Lauts, J. *Carpaccio*, Oxford 1962.

Mâle, E. *L'Art religieux du XIIe siècle en France*, Paris 1922.

L'Art religieux du XIIIe siècle en France, Paris 1898.

Religious art from the twelfth to the eighteenth century, Princeton 1982.

Bibliography

'Etudes sur l'art de l'époque romane', *Revue de Paris*, année 28, no. 3, 1 er & 15 juin 1921, pp. 491–513 & 711–32.

Mariacher, G. *Mosaici di San Marco*, Venezia 1980.

Il Sansovino, Milano 1962.

Morris, J. *Venice*, London 1960.

The Venetian Empire, London 1980.

Moschini, V. *La leggenda di Sant' Orsola*, Milano 1957.

Murray, P. *The Architecture of the Italian Renaissance*, London 1969.

Norwich, J. J. *Venice: the rise to Empire*, London 1977.

Venice: the Greatness and Fall, London 1981.

Padoue: itinéraires touristiques, Venezia 1970.

Palucchini, R. *I teleri di Carpaccio alla Scuola San Giorgio degli Schiavoni*, Milano 1961.

Panofsky, E. *Meaning in the Visual Arts*, New York 1955.

Peroccho, G. *La Confrérie des Saints Georges et Tryphon. Guide de l'Ecole San Giorgio degli Schiavoni*, Venezia 1964.

Ragg, L. & L. M. *Things Seen in Venice*, London 1913.

Rice, D. T. *Art of the Byzantine Era*, London 1963.

Ruskin, J. *Works* (Library Edition), London 1903–12.

St. Mark's Rest, Orpington 1877–9.

The Stones of Venice, 3 vols. & General Index, London 1851–6 & 1886.

The Stones of Venice (Traveller's Edition), Orpington 1879–81.

The Stones of Venice (ed. J. Morris), London 1981.

Ruskin's Venice (ed. A. Whittick), London 1976.

de Sanchez Rivero, A. M. *Quattro Spagnoli in Venezia*, Venezia 1957.

Serres, M. *Esthétiques sur Carpaccio*, Paris 1975.

de la Sizeranne, R. *Ruskin ou la religion de la beauté*, Paris 1897.

Stubblebine J. (ed.), *Giotto: the Arena Chapel Frescoes*, New York 1969.

Valcanover, F. *Le gallerie della Accademia*, Venezia 1981.

Valsecchi, M. *Cappella degli Scrovegni*, Novara 1962.

Venise: guide complet en couleurs, Venezia 1978.

Vergilius Maro, P. *Aeneid*, book VIII, ed. K. W. Gransden, Cambridge 1976.

Werdnig, G. *Die Osellen oder Münz-Medaillen der Republik Venedig*, Wien 1889.

Winternitz, E. *Musical Instruments and their Symbolism in Western Art*, London 1967.

Index

Index

Index

Index